FROM RIOT TO REASON

From Riot
to Reason

ELDON L. JOHNSON

UNIVERSITY OF ILLINOIS PRESS

Urbana
Chicago
London

The substance of Chapter Two first appeared in
Colleges and Universities as Agents of Social Change,
Western Interstate Commission for Higher Education,
Boulder, Colorado, 1968.

CHAPTER ONE

The Crisis of Confidence

Universities must pull themselves together. That is the dominant refrain of the report of the President's Commission on Campus Unrest. It is said no less than three times.

That admonition contains a damning judgment: universities have come apart, disintegrated. This is surely an unprecedented evaluation in the history of American education. Therefore, it is time to look into causes and remedies.

Universities are suffering from unrelenting criticism. Their purposes are called into question and their motives suspect. Their objectivity is under attack and their integrity assailed. They are accused of being improvident, custom-caked, and arrogant. They are under suspicion of harboring students who are troublemakers, defending faculty who are irresponsible, and lacking courage to clean up the resulting "mess." Some of this

I

impression rests on lack of information, some on mis-information, and all of it is somehow grounded in what the President's Commission calls the "crisis of under-standing."

The times are novel. The President of the nation has repeatedly singled out the universities for official comment and for special investigation. He has made policy statements about university disorders through official governmental channels; repeatedly commented in press conferences, campaign speeches, and nation-wide television broadcasts; publicly corresponded and conversed with professors and students; and even named a special short-term White House advisor on campus unrest. After six student deaths at the hands of public agents at Kent State University and Jackson State College, he appointed the Commission on Campus Unrest to be chaired by former Governor William W. Scranton of Pennsylvania. Paralleling President Johnson's naming of the Kerner Commission on civil disorders, the need felt for the Scranton Commission two years later shows the ascendancy which campus problems have reached in the public mind — a shift from riots on the streets to trouble on the campus. Also writing a new chapter in American history, the Vice-President of the United States joined many senators and representatives of both political parties in making campus problems a major campaign issue in the elec-

2

tions of 1970. Restrictive, remedial, and sometimes punitive congressional action has been profusely proposed and a modest amount actually enacted. For universities to be national news, national politics, congressional target, and presidential preoccupation is a far cry from the older constitutional view that public responsibility for education should be borne at the state level. Such is the unhappy status of universities nowadays, at least as viewed by a substantial part of the population.

The picture at the state and local political levels and in the mass media is all too familiar. Polls show campus unrest is viewed as the nation's No. 2 problem. This is again unique in the annals of colleges and universities. The problem is not simply that the public do not understand. They do not trust. They have lost their traditional faith in higher education. It is a crisis of confidence as well as a crisis of understanding, and it does not follow that restoring the understanding will automatically restore the confidence. Only the internal partisans of the university itself, and rather blind ones at that, can feel assured that acquaintance with all the cold, unadulterated facts will ipso facto restore confidence. It will take more — the erasure of one image and the incremental building of another by a different kind of performance. There is no camera which can be clicked to produce an instantaneous new image.

The crisis of confidence has many roots. The taproot is violence — violence led by college and university youth. This has captured the headlines and both alienated and alarmed the public, as it has also "turned off" a substantial portion of the student population who for the first time began to see clearly where their dissent would have to stop. Violence is violence, and any of it is too much. So the image of pampered youth biting the hand that feeds them and destroying what they above all others should cherish is not easily moderated by cold statistics showing that only 5 percent of the four-year campuses and 17 percent of the universities experienced violence and only a small minority of students actually were involved. There are other statistics. For the first time in the history of the listing of the "Ten Most Wanted Criminals" by the Federal Bureau of Investigation, the majority are young radicals with immediate university connections. In fact, there are nine of this type out of the sixteen on the expanded "most wanted" list, including three women, a former university newspaper editor, a black student organizer, and leaders of the Students for a Democratic Society. Again, allegations that the FBI is engaged in systematic repression of youthful radicalism will not cause the public to forget or condone the crimes which are committed — arson, rioting, sabotage, and bombings, with resulting deaths in some cases. The killings at Kent

4

State and Jackson State — students in their "sanctuary" yet shot by outside "officers of the law" — likewise have their complexities which will never be generally and fully comprehended, but most of the onlookers via the mass media believe that where there is smoke there is also fire. It is that simple, and the universities are that simply involved. The more recent campus move from mass rioting to individual acts of terrorism has shaken public confidence even more. Guerrilla action is hardest to cope with and is designed to breed and spread not just fear, but panic. This is the current phase of the evolution of campus violence, and not much besides total conflagration could be better designed to spoil the image of universities.

Another factor in the undermining of confidence is the impression, as most of the public see it, that universities have lost control of their own affairs. Things have fallen apart. No one is in charge. Factions flourish. The boat in which all students find themselves is rudderless. It threatens to become a derelict and may have to be seized for the safety of others. Indecision is rife. Witness the hesitation, waiting for polls, referrals, debates, conferences, consensuses, on such seemingly uncomplicated commonsense matters as whether student arms are appropriate on campus, whether police should ever be called, whether employers should have recruitment access to the campus,

5

whether amnesty is an appropriate judgment on accused students, and whether professors may unilaterally alter their terms of employment. The university never got much public mileage out of its proud claim to academic freedom — strained acceptance yes, but never solid acclaim — but it now suffers immeasurably when students make a whimsical, self-righteous determination of who may speak and who may not. Unlike the old episodes about unsavory characters who were invited to appear, the tables have now turned and the "most respectable" people are sometimes kept from speaking on campus — the Secretary of State or Defense, the Vice-President, or a southern senator. Again, these are minority episodes, quite atypical, but they convey the message not lost on the already shaken public. How can a university which asks for self-determination put up with such a travesty of the freedom it proclaims, and which it professes to serve as guardian?

Another factor is the new deglamourized public expectations of the university. The old deference is gone. The university is no longer the intellectual church. Instead, it is a burgeoning behemoth with an insatiable appetite for tuition and tax dollars. In some states, even wealthy ones, higher education is taking as much as 25 percent of the total revenue collected by the state government. The increasing budgetary competition with other government departments leads to the facile conclusion that the public university is or ought to be "just another government department," with exactly the same kind of close accountability. Also, university education has become common. When more than 50 percent of college-age youth go on to higher education, the impression of a changed university role is hardly avoidable. Every "kid next door" is going, and he is not ordinarily an ambassador of glamour and intellectual power. Nevertheless, the egalitarian sentiments of the public nowadays call for more wide-open educational opportunity, less boasting of the numbers turned away, more admission of blacks and disadvantaged, and other "leveling" characteristics which undercut the traditional grounds for trusting the aloof university. The high-brow role no longer charms. Likewise, professors are no longer the remote, robed elite they once were. They inhabit every junior college district and they are many times as numerous as when the parents of university students were growing up. Their feet of clay show in the news, in the supermarket, and in everyday local controversies. To cap the growing impression, professors are beginning to unionize, just like the plumbers, auto workers, and truck drivers. Confidence in the intellectual clergy is thus put under some added strain.

The university is also widely regarded as indifferent to society. It is insensitive and unresponsive. Professors have always wanted to be men apart. They expect to be paid without awareness of who pays; hence they seem not only to be without helpfulness but also without gratitude. They are either doing research in place of teaching or research without payoff in practical terms. Much of government's disenchantment with higher education rests on the notion that the huge investment in academic research has not yielded adequate dividends. What society wants in direct intellectual help it has to get increasingly from non-university sources — think tanks, consulting firms, foundations, and private contractors. None of this builds confidence in the university as a willing partner, as a reservoir of talent on tap, or as an institution vested with a public interest. Compounding this disillusionment is the impression that the university caught up in violence and disruption wants to be left alone at precisely the points where the public is disposed to move in.

Finally, lack of confidence in the university stems from an all-pervasive concern about youth. The defects and dangers associated with youth and youthful action are in turn linked with the universities. When the student style is to shock and challenge, and even to dictate and destroy, the practitioners of the style and the institutions which they inhabit are bound to be in disrepute with those who are shocked, challenged, or injured.

The university can easily be seen as an accomplice with youth in attempting to live life without consequences. This coupled with some visible faculty alliances with "the oppositional college student subculture" makes a heady potion for public consumption, and the blurred vision which ensues does not nicely discriminate between the offending minority and the orthodox majority. Likewise, the dogfight between the radical extremes of left and right, agreeing on the evils of the university but for opposite reasons, easily accentuates and confirms the fears of the middle masses.

What can be done about this erosion of confidence is an exceedingly complicated business. It is tantamount to asking what should be done about universities in general, now that they are in crisis. Perhaps the prescription of the Scranton Report is as good as any — "universities must pull themselves together." This implies restoration, reconciliation, and presumably change and improvement in the process. Selected aspects of this response to the crisis of understanding are the subjects of these essays.

Two matters need immediate and undergirding attention: renewed awareness of the strengths and essential characteristics of the American university, and a clarification and revalidation of its mission. What the university has too long taken for granted, even among its own members, to say nothing of a more remote pub-

9

lic, needs reexamination. As Justice Oliver Wendell Holmes has said, "at this time we need education in the obvious more than investigation of the obscure."

So much has been said about what is wrong with universities that the time has come to ask what is right. In other words, what is solid enough and central enough to be preserved as the core, however much other changes may need to occur?

Above all, the university is the special sanctuary of reason and reflection. It is society's only institution which specializes in critical thinking as a way of life. It is the domicile of the nation's intellectuals and the chief source of its intellectual progress. In that domicile there are the scientists and leaders of the professions, the high priests of research, the experts, the social critics, the trustees of human knowledge, and the philosophers, historians, and other humanists who live by contemplation and teaching. There are the Nobel laureates. There are the makers of books. There are the masters of those arts which are too delicate for the marketplace. There are the librarians and their great collections, the envy of academics around the world. All this is what makes universities exciting places for those associated with them. There have been times in human history when the mainstream of intellectual life existed outside the universities. Despite some new inroads in this direction, the center of gravity is still on the campus, and the more basic or fundamental the need, the greater the certainty of campus domicile. The university has been the home of breakthroughs in space, in prolongation of life, and in harnessing the atom. Its academic science is deservedly the envy of the world. Even some history-turning public policies have had academic authorship, such as the social security system begun in the 1930's. In an age increasingly dependent on knowledge, the custodianship of learning, with the recruitment and nurturing of "those who know," is a monumental contribution.

At the other extreme, concerning what is immediate and practical, higher education has provided, with great dependability, the certification of the manpower needed by industry, government, and the professions. This is an indispensable service in the elaborate division of labor by which modern society lives. It is also a welcome contribution to further national development and economic growth. It has done in America that which the developing countries abroad are always trying to emulate. It has established education as a social investment, not a mere consumer good to be bought in the market by those who are able. As some youthful critics are quick to point out, manpower preparation may be the quintessence of serving "the establishment," but even the post-establishment — whatever that will be — will have to have educated manpower, however different the content. Preparing for the professions as they are, while leading them to improvement, is not a bad university role, and however short the universities may fall in specific instances, they generally aspire both to serve and to change. Standing at the gate to all the major professions and holding the preparatory key to the nation's myriad high-level positions, the universities have done nothing else so confidently as to supply the personnel market, or whatever more euphemistic title one wants to give the matching of talent and skills with socially needed services. This is the university's greatest quantitative achievement, and judging from the comparative standing of the American professions and the performance of the employing organizations, quality has not been lacking. This is surely something that is basically right with universities.

The university is also basically right in its signal contribution to social mobility. An open society prides itself on permitting everyone to rise to the level of his potentiality — to show how great a distance he can go from the equal start he had with everyone else. How to start with students where they are and elevate their status in life has been a kind of specialty of colleges and universities in America. Many of them were regarded as inferior because they rated so badly by ideal standards; yet they could and did exceed the standards and lift the achievements of those they served — the members of their church, the youth of their race, the students of their region. The explicit extension of opportunities for breaking the racial barriers is the latest, if belated, projection of our "religion" of the redemptive value of education, which has now opened college and university doors to a greater number and wider spread of youth than anywhere else. Eight percent of the university-age group is enrolled in West Germany and 14 percent in France and Great Britain, as compared to 50 percent in the United States, with more than 75 percent in Utah and California. Indeed a new voice in the land — or an ancient voice with new vigor — begins to cry that we have gone too far. Nevertheless, the matching of opportunity with talent and the lifting of realizable economic and social sights are the essentials of the American dynamic, which securely rests on open and ready access to higher education.

To their immense but often forgotten credit, colleges and universities have doggedly sustained whatever is left of the notion that man should be prepared to live as well as to work — that culture is needed as well as fact, that the specialized should be grounded in the general, and that the humane values for directing knowledge must supplement knowledge itself. From the student slogans in the streets, one might conclude that this is exactly what is missing from the academic scene; but where among universities around the world

is there anything like the American prolongation of
liberal education? Whether, as alleged, it exists to pro-
long adolescence or to keep youth out of the labor
market, it does exist; and it just might be that it exists
because most academics still believe in it. This is where
the independent colleges, as distinguished from the universities, have made signal contribution; but even the
latter are now articulating the need for synthesis and
wholeness, as shown in the emphasis on "ecological,"
"environmental," "comparative," and "interdisciplin-
ary." The current move away from "general education" does not negate the point made here because
almost all reformers are still pleading for non-speciali-
zation at the undergraduate level, however changed
the forms may be. When the commission headed by
Lord Robbins made recommendations for revolutionary changes in British university education a few years
ago, it spoke with envy of the breadth-depth balance
and the postponement of specialization in American
university education. This feature, taken too much for
granted, was singled out for emulation.

Universities have also become the patrons of the
arts. Some contend that the American theater has gone
to the country — academic country, particularly —
and that it will be saved there, if at all. Museums and
galleries always piggy-backed on colleges and universities, even in the most unlikely places, almost as

certainly as public libraries followed Andrew Carnegie's dollars. Poets-in-residence and painters-in-residence now enrich university life, plus the community. It may be a little florid to say that the universities are the Lorenzos and the popes of contemporary art patronage, but the analogy is not inapt within current egalitarianism. Furthermore, the special academic impact in the arts has been at the growing edge — the experimental. In collecting and publishing books, higher education also excels, as it likewise sustains many of the journals which conduct scholarly discourse around the globe.

While intellectually organized and administered around disciplines, the American college and even the university have also been strongly student-centered. Student dissatisfaction, however otherwise justified, cannot deny or ignore the point: in comparison to academic life elsewhere in the world, the student here is central and favored. He has direct and ready access to his professors, with no barrier of status and protocol. He has entirely atypical freedom in his choice of courses, and has had ever since President Eliot of Harvard introduced free electives as a panacea. Libraries are for the student's use, usually with open access and reading space intermingled with books. Student unions have long facilitated his common life. The straitjacket of examinations has never erased his second and third chances. And the rigidity of "faculties" has not barred changes of mind and of career preparation. He has never been subjected to the system of part-time professors with major employment off campus. He was the first in the world to have not minimal but elaborate student services: placement, counseling, financial aids, activity planning, and health clinics, culminating in deanships and vice-presidencies wholly student-oriented. If some of this led to smothering paternalism, that description no longer holds. Students have always counted but never so much as today, in the wake of their insistence that they *be* counted.

Universities have also successfully insisted on sufficient autonomy to guarantee freedom of inquiry and social criticism. There have been failures, institutionally and in celebrated individual cases, but the generalization holds. The record is not bad. This means having fended off the tight control of the state or the interference of philanthropy. The accusations of academic heresy and the demands for academic punishment are never absent, itself a sure sign that capitulation has not been made. The freedom of the professor to teach and to research and the freedom of the student to learn and to dissent are never out of danger, sometimes inside, but usually outside, the institution. The freedom fighters have historically been determined faculties, firm administrators, and courageous trustees. When the chips are down, the ferocity of the faculties, if hard pressed, has been the decisive factor. As sanctuaries for highly educated men and women who do not want to go either into business or into exile, as one historian put it, the universities have preserved their internal freedom and even dared to speak not only as the nation's intellect but sometimes also as its conscience.

Finally, there is a summarizing, overall fact which has far-reaching implications: American higher education is making a significant impact elsewhere in the world. It is one of our chief items of cultural export. Many new nations are enthusiastic, satisfied customers, not as mimics but as discriminating users. More foreign students come to America than to any other nation. Furthermore, among those attracted in growing numbers are graduate and advanced professional students, presumably the most sophisticated and knowledgeable in their capacity to appraise educational systems. America is especially sought after by post-doctoral fellows, young men and women who are ambitious for educational topping-off abroad, much as young American intellectuals went to Germany a century ago. The American appeal, ironically, is greatest at the point so often criticized at home — the graduate level, the most specialized, the most research-oriented. In fact, the filling of their faculties with U.S.-trained scholars has become a lively issue in Canadian universities. The brain drain of senior scientists to this country has been debated in the British House of Commons. Our colleges and universities have come a long way since Lord Bryce, British ambassador to the United States in the 1880's, struggled so hard to find hope in them, in that celebrated chapter of *The American Commonwealth*.

These, then, despite the risks of overgeneralization and exaggeration by emphasis, are some of the strengths and virtues which university personnel too much assume and too little articulate. They are merits of which the outside critics are commonly ignorant. In fact, such critics are often, unwittingly, asking the universities to be more fully what they already are — and the universities might well take that advice. They have values and services worthy of preserving as the nuclei around which almost infinite variations and experimentation can be launched for improvement, and should be. Both internally and externally, the university task in the crisis of confidence is twofold: to defend and conserve but also to criticize and change.

Another drag upon confidence would be removed if the mission of the university were more clearly agreed upon, articulated, and generally understood. There is less agreement now than ever before. More kinds of institutions represent more missions, even if they have a common core. Faculty and students have widely divergent views. Students disagree among themselves — graduate and undergraduate students, liberal arts and engineering students, residential and extension students. The public is prone to want everything simultaneously and indiscriminately. The radicals want to "bring it to a grinding halt," without any clue as to where the presumed new start would lead. Complaints are common against "too much research," "neglected teaching," and "being all things to all people."

The stock answer to the question of university mission is commitment to the acquisition, dissemination, and application of knowledge — the familiar triad of research, teaching, and service — but this needs clarification. Controversy rages about the proportions in the mix and, in particular, about the propriety and nature of "service," if it is in fact valid as a separate function.

The starting point needing steady repetition for public consumption is the awareness that the university is an intellectual institution. It deals in knowledge. Its mission cannot legitimately get off that track. So acquiring knowledge and disseminating it are central. What is already known has to be transmitted to those who do not yet know it. The continuity of the culture is paramount. That part is the teaching task. It is the highest priority in the sense that if all university functions were dropped one by one, proceeding downward from that which is least fundamental to survival, teaching would be the last leaf on the tree. The heritage must go on — or no one would be prepared to do research or to perform service. The skills of society would atrophy and disappear. Not only must students be taught but other teachers must be prepared. College professors must reproduce themselves also. Yet, ironically, this conception of the university's mission — the centrality of teaching — would be questioned less outside the university than within it. The simplistic outside view is likely to overstate the assumption of the near-monopoly of teaching. But the fact is that, contrary to this view, the percentage of floor space devoted to classrooms and other strictly teaching activities is shockingly small in the large universities. It may be less than 10 percent. This is not proof that teaching is underemphasized: research is a voracious and disproportionate consumer of space. But it is an indication of need for a better balanced view of the university's mission, at least as presently conceived, even after conceding the bedrock position of teaching.

Discovery is another university role, adding to the corpus of knowledge. To what is known and can be taught to others who do not yet know there must be added the knowledge which no one had previously known, not even professors. This research role is the special task of the university as distinguished from most colleges, because research itself is a mode of teaching the next generation of scholars; it relies on the "knowledge bank" represented by libraries, computers, laboratories, and scholars; and it is a way of leading the great professions rather than being intellectually indentured to them by simple manpower training. The university's relation to knowledge is not merely custodial: it is regenerative and seminal.

The popular on-campus and off-campus sport of deriding research as if it could be dispensed with needs to be exposed and repudiated. The university is not like a fountain continually recirculating a fixed supply of water. Wellsprings are needed. Graduate education calls for research as a method of learning, for research as the rejuvenative force in the faculty, and for research as the source of change, even in what to teach. Students, public, and politicians who want only a "teaching institution," meaning without research, do not know what it takes to teach in a university. This central point must somehow be sorted out and distinguished from the legitimate and unending debate about what *proportion* of institutional time should be devoted to research and what research is *in fact* significantly relevant to teaching. There can be no doubt that some academics can and do overstate and overwork their research claims, but the current danger comes from the other side — from the critics who think the simplistic solution to campus unrest is to throttle university research.

After having said that the university's mission must be grounded in teaching and research, it is apparent that something else remains. Should there be teaching outside the campus classroom, and some of it quite informally, for those who long ago finished college, for those who quit to work, or for those who want the university to share what it knows about their daily occupations? Should the university do that kind of off-campus "teaching" which is consulting, conferring, or counseling? Also, should there be research which is applied to practical problem-solving for the community, government, or industry? In other words, is there a legitimate service function too? Obviously the university, if it wishes, can have an outreach role which extends its capacity to off-campus clients. It can have extended teaching and extended research. To ask "Should it?" in the contemporary world seems strange indeed, but the crisis of confidence has sharply raised precisely that question, which must now be faced.

The President's Commission on Campus Unrest has given its answer, although an equivocal one. At first blush, the conclusion seems clear enough in the references to the "primary missions of teaching and research," to the "university's core functions," and to service activities labeled as "peripheral." Even more explicit is the summary: "In general, we recommend reduction of outside service commitments." It turns out, however, as so often is the case, that the definition of "service" is the troublemaker. The Commission goes on to hedge by saying teaching and research *are* service. It also wants to get the universities out of those "service relationships [which] are now a major source of income," which comes to mean defense-related research. The possible proscription of ROTC programs is also mentioned. These matters, however, are not "service" at all in the sense conceived by universities which have singled out a special type of work for extension or public-service personnel. The activities condemned or questioned are certain kinds of research and certain kinds of teaching. The semantic difficulty gets worse when the report says, "as universities reduce their *extraneous* service commitments, they must also search for *new ways to serve* by relating their policies, programs, and expertise to pressing local and national problems." A long list of possible local involvements follows, from "direct health services" and "field work" for students to, surprisingly, the sponsoring of federal programs of housing and equal opportunity. In view of this devotion to one kind of service but not another, one is forced to conclude that the Commission was understandably preoccupied with campus unrest, and on that ground, in search of remedy, it sought quick relief from the tribulations of defense research and ROTC, both tied to a controversial federal policy overseas. In so doing, with the apparent outlawry of what is called "service," the report compounds the problem of defining more sharply the university mission. It has unwittingly supplied a bludgeon which will beat legitimate university activities over the head for a long time to come, including its own desiderata of more voluntarism in education and of more "relevance."

The service role of the university is its most misunderstood role. Its legitimacy cannot be denied on the ground that teaching *is* service and research *is* service. What the statement should say is that teaching or research *can* be service. Making it so is one of the university's special tasks. Educating youth who will in turn perform service to society and doing research which someone else can apply to problems is neither all the university can do nor what it ought to do. If it is the custodian of human knowledge and is manned by specialized experts, what decrees that all this must be reserved for residential students in the magical years required for formal degrees, with the remainder of society spurned? Rooted in society, supported by society, accountable to society, the university is the instrument for intellectual service, in whatever way knowledge can be brought to bear. Discovering knowledge is one way. Passing it on to learners is another.

Applying it to problems is still another, more important than ever before. In the lingo of the day, knowledge needs a "delivery system." It is not adequate in the test tube and the classroom — not adequate for the problems of the world and the citizens who face them (while supporting higher education) and, equally important, not adequate for those who man the test tubes and the classrooms.

This comes to the crux of the matter. Service is essential to complete the articulated teaching-research-service cycle, or to round out what can and ought to be an integrated system. It is illuminating and evaluative for the researcher and teacher, as well as useful to the outside customer. Service has an organic connection with instruction and research which makes excision a threat to the health of the whole university body. Application of knowledge to the world's needs provides the feedback which redirects future research and future teaching, like the automatic retargeting of an artillery piece in action. Knowledge not put to use or brought to some point is not complete. As research enriches teaching, service adds something to both — the test of relevance, the freshness of immediacy, and the antidote for myopic specialization. To repeat, service is essential to the recycling of knowledge through creation, dissemination, application, and then more creation in the light of experience. This is as essential

25

to the university in doing what it professes as it is to society in getting what it expects. And that mutuality of interest is the real test of what service the university should undertake.

It would be unconscionable for the university in its time of greatest crisis, with its loss of public understanding, to act as if it has nothing to say to, or to do for, the outside men and groups who are working on problems of war overseas, race relations at home, environment in the cities, mid-career obsolescence in the professions, or delivery of decent health care to everybody. This is inevitably a time of greater faculty involvement, of "being where the action is," of student exposure to off-campus realities, of use of the cities as social laboratories, and of fitting the university more closely to the contemporary world. If it makes a significant difference for a university to be located in crisis-ridden Nigeria or India, it also makes an enormous difference for a university to be located in contemporary crisis-ridden America. Simply to say all will teach and do research misses the crucial context which imparts life, relevance, and distinction. It neglects much that will restore confidence.

Two caveats are in order. The President's Commission on Campus Unrest warns that service nowadays tends to run to the controversial and hence toward politicizing the university. This is a danger, and par-

ticularly for the publicly supported university; but
there are academic techniques for entering into policy-
laden questions (e.g., the unresolved matters, hence
controversial) without being compromisingly "political." Likewise, the university should not assume outreach obligations which are devoid of professional
payoff, doing nothing for teaching or research or
striking no professional fire in the breasts of the faculty participants. Furthermore, the academic community is so sensitized to institutional autonomy and
professional independence that the reflex from the hot
stove of controversy will be a powerful countervailing
force against unwise service, even when vehemently
urged by campus militants. The politicizing danger is
real, although it can be a cover-up for excessive cau-
tion. Nevertheless, its probable incidence in particular
cases has to be weighed. The second caveat: generali-
zations about "the university" obscure the great diversity in American higher education. There will be equal
diversity in precise institutional missions. The particular mix of research, teaching, and service has to be
agreed upon within each institution in its own terms.
The service component, for example, makes a larger
claim on the public university than the private, the
urban institution than the "college on the hill," the
graduate than undergraduate level, the technologically
oriented school than the liberal arts type. But no in-

27

stitution can ignore Alfred North Whitehead's well-known attack upon "inert ideas," knowledge conceived as not useful, and "the deadly harm . . . done to young minds . . . by depreciation of the present." If, as he says, "Education is the acquisition of the art of the utilization of knowledge," why should the university be so reluctant to seize the immense opportunities which lie around it? The time has come for universities to accept full membership in society, to throw more bridges over the moat, and to invite greater two-way traffic.

"The crisis on American campuses has no parallel in the history of the nation. This crisis has roots in divisions of American society as deep as any since the Civil War." This is frightening language from the President's Commission on Campus Unrest. While they should not be the scapegoat for the nation's ills, the universities plainly have their own work to do. They have not made clear the relation between their problems and society's problems, and the differences. Indeed, they have hardly taken the initiative at all, even to explain themselves — including their values, their contributions, their indispensable ambience, and their mission. Explication will not suffice, of course. What is perceived is as important as what is. Therefore, the university has the awesome task of seeing that there is a closer fit between education and the ongoing social revolution and finding tangible and convincing ways of *demonstrating* that congruence.

CHAPTER TWO

Confrontation: University and Public

THE UNIVERSITY cannot be the cutting edge of change without encountering resistance from the materials it threatens to cut. A dynamic tension between the university and its environment is normal, but the current face-off between university and public is cause for concern. The trend is even ominous. Society is becoming more avaricious and demanding in its consumption of university services. The university is becoming more willing to put down its walls, to be where the action is, to criticize public policy, and even to risk confusing power with influence. This mutual interpenetration creates more points of friction and more promise of conflict.

The central issue is not new. Whether the freedom enjoyed within the campus can be extended outside the campus bothered universities centuries ago. Social criticism and public service as university functions have been growing for almost a century. Catering to clients as well as to students and serving as the arm of government have long and respectable traditions in land-grant universities. Whether freedom of action extends as far as freedom of thought, and whether professors enjoy the same latitude off the campus as on, have long troubled the academic waters. When is a campus a legitimate sanctuary and when a revolutionary cell? When does sponsored research seduce the university? To what extent should the university be the agent of government? When can the university countenance the disobeying of the law? Is neutrality really an endorsement of a rotten society? All or most of these questions were current before contemporary students added their flamboyant provocation. Whether these youth are the "new fascisti," nihilists, or genuine agents of change, they evoke images of what is inside the walls, ready to spill out on an innocent society when the university talks of its extramural mission. Political forays, disruption, violence, and other direct actionism from universities in Europe and Latin America, now brought home by America's own surprising excesses, have etched the image more deeply.

But the underlying issue persists: How can the university retain the freedom it requires from a society it criticizes? How can it retain its competence and its capacity to affect the course of society without incurring hostility from a society content with its course? There is where the crunch comes. The sleeping issue is now shouting at us.

The university exists on the sufferance of the state. As Karl Jaspers has said: "Its existence is dependent on political considerations. It can only live where and as the state desires. . . . Society wants the university because it feels that the pure service of truth somewhere within its orbit serves its own interests." But the service of God is offensive to the devil. The pursuit of truth inevitably leads to controversy about both the truth and its consequences. Hence it is not surprising to note that Professor Walter P. Metzger, historian of academic freedom, concludes that it takes great vision for "any society, interested in the immediate goals of solidarity and self-preservation," to subsidize free criticism and inquiry. The accommodation which persists in our universities is "one of the remarkable achievements of man," although "one cannot but be appalled at the slender thread by which it hangs."

In this precarious balance, society has come to adopt some pragmatic tolerances. It is accustomed to extension activities, to service bureaus, to contractual relations with government, and to overseas assistance. The pre–Civil War college related only modestly to the limited professional life of that time and hardly at all to science, technology, business, and agriculture. In contrast, higher education today is actively serving these, plus government itself, on a host of fronts, and with public acceptance. But the "slender thread" begins to appear when unorthodox or politically sensitive activities are attempted, even under these tolerances — activities such as university implementation of the U.S. Department of Agriculture's social policies, legal aid services, dispensing of contraceptives in the university medical clinics, service overseas for the Central Intelligence Agency, leadership training for civil rights workers, or urban renewal assistance. The slender thread is further attenuated when faculty and students resort, as some are now advocating, to a host of direct-action measures to challenge "the establishment," to appeal to "the higher law" of conscience, and to dramatize social ills thought to be too urgent to wait upon persuasion. Indeed, the object has sometimes become precisely that of straining the tolerances of society; and that can easily be done by anti-war stances, formally adopted manifestos for social reform, preferential graduate admissions of draft resisters, occupation and obstruction of public buildings, insistence on fixed quotas for the employment of minority groups, defiance of the police, memorializing for "pot" and "pill," aiding Cuba, making alliances with the black nationalists, and doing much else which anyone can add from his own home experience. These are the shouts and sharp blows of the Karate Age, as someone has called it, perhaps unwittingly to contrast it to the whimperings of the bygone Aspirin Age.

What are the stakes in this new confrontation? What is placed in jeopardy? Most obviously, the freedom of the university itself from outside interference; in other words, society's acceptance of the university as an objective intellectual force, possessed of integrity and competent to be a social critic. Most directly at stake is the survival of the activist role the university community professes; but more important, at stake is the university's moderate and necessary participative social role, which is required for maintaining relevance in what it teaches, what it investigates, and what it extends to the outside world. The hard-to-defend jeopardizes the defensible. At stake is the whole interconnecting apparatus between the university and society, the apparatus through which meaningful communication takes place, balance is attained, accommodation is achieved, and mutual dependence is acknowledged.

Who is affected? Who gets involved? Who produces the consequences? Four audiences or potential respondents may be identified: the external academic world, the mass media, the general public, and the government.

The external academic community, consisting of

the lower educational institutions, other universities and their faculties, professional societies, and accrediting bodies, is such an "in" group, so sympathetic and understanding that it would rarely present any consequences or sanctions. An exception might arise from one of the professional societies which takes its cue from its practitioners and feels possessive about the educational production of new colleagues and competitors. Accrediting bodies, unlike the general public, would probably regard extreme institutional activism as an acceptable additive unless it patently threatened to disrupt and despoil the teaching and research functions. Extreme university activism might alienate counselors in high schools and junior colleges, with enrollment effects. However, generally speaking, fellow educators outside the university would be hard to alienate. Since they have neither disposition nor organization for sanction, they may be eliminated as a significant factor.

The next audience, the mass media, is of vital concern. Its impact is great. It goes about its professional job, as it sees it, paying little or no attention to the consequences, but leaving that to the public in the way that science leaves its capacity for evil as well as good. Virtually every opportunity the university has to reach the general public, as distinguished from selected groups like the alumni, is through the mass media. This includes what the university itself supplies, what reporters uncover, or what unexpectedly explodes into newsworthiness, however much the explosion might have been engineered precisely to capture headlines. Since the nature of news — except that concerning the political, social, business, athletic, and entertainment elites — is that which is aberrant, unusual, extreme, or unrepeatable, social activism on the part of the university, or its faculty or students, is likely to get unusual coverage. Such activism produces adversary relations, on which journalism thrives. The approach usually is, What is the score? Who is winning?

Paradoxically, the university itself is also a communications institution. Its success depends on the free flow of ideas in the scholarly community, and among scholars outside, with only minor spill-over to the general public. However, the trend toward more activism and more direct outside involvement inevitably puts the university into the arena covered by mass communications rather than by scholarly discourse. So the university will become increasingly subject to the major limitation of the mass media: the necessary presentation of selective evidence. Complex problems, which activist positions usually represent, inevitably suffer when stripped to simplistic interpretations, overcompression, or one-facet coverage. Likewise, the university which is tied to the complex problems also suffers as the reading or listening public makes up its mind on the basis of inadequate perception. Getting the facts is no doubt a scrupulously held journalistic objective, but space dictates selectivity and readership dictates appeal to the mass. Ample examples show how the ripple can be made a tide, the amusing made menacing, the minority made a majority, the conscientious made unconscionable, and the compromise made a capitulation.

When to these natural news limitations of the mass media are added the editorial policies of commentators and publishers — policies based on their own news coverage plus their personal predilections — the university must seriously reckon with this pervasive prism, yielding both color and heat, which stands between it and its other publics. No conceivable crisis of activism can escape the influence of public scrutiny via press, radio, and television. No one has. No one will. This is the price an activist university must be prepared to pay. It may win journalistic allies or enemies, but it will not be ignored.

Another maker of consequences is the general public — all readers and listeners of the mass media, including the alumni, the benefactors, the consumers (such as extension clients, contractors, and parents of students), and those who are uninterested and unaffected until some university act or policy welds them into some new pro- or anti-university "public." This is the most potent university audience, in one sense, but it is also an object of much democratic folklore. It makes public opinion. It helps evaluate what ought to become public policy. It dictates to government. But it cannot rise above the sources of its information, which for the individual reader or listener is not only selective but largely monopolized. It is subject, as Walter Lippmann used to say, to the pictures in the head — not only the accumulated encrustation of values and prejudices through which all supposed fact is screened but also the pictures which are newly being built by the persistent impact of the news media. In this context, the university is what the public *thinks* it is. Fact is not as important as the perception of fact, unless one can find some independent way to appeal to fact, to make it real again.

Within "*the* public" are subordinate publics, some closely allied to the university and with which it may have special ways of maintaining the liaison — such as alumni publications, special releases to select lists, offices concentrated on benefactions, and communications with the professional groups standing behind the university's professional schools. But the more important question is what makes a "public" for the university. Such a group has to arise out of a perceived interest — maybe a threat, maybe a cause to join —

which is keenly enough felt to inspire action. This public-generating capacity exists in unusual degree in activist programs. This is where the patriotic groups are galvanized into action, the interest groups become defensive, the power-threatened retaliate, the neighborhood reacts to the intruding university, the outraged religious sects are heard from, and the forgotten group is inspired to shout. It is only a step from the birth of such publics to their appeal to public action through public officers, for punishment or for favor.

This then leads to the last and most potent maker of consequences: government. This is where the university, whether public or private, meets its greatest potential enemy, as it may likewise be a potential benefactor. Government can change the rules of the game or call for a new game. Its restraint is what makes the university possible: its not doing what it clearly could do. Therefore, the university which wants to participate in matters the government also cares about, the great public-policy questions, will have to take the government very much into account — government as an ally, as a supporter, as a protector; or as a score-evener, as an enemy, as an intruder, as a seducer. The university will have to measure its moderation/aggression scale alongside the government's tolerance/retaliation scale. This means local, state, and national governments, and the executive, legislative, and judicial branches. All levels and all branches have recently demonstrated their capacity to embarrass, to restrain, and to punish higher education if the provocation is deemed sufficient.

In view of the roles of these three particularly potent university "publics," the question is, What consequences can these makers of consequences produce?

The mass media can obviously help manufacture all the other publics; but they can also themselves oppose bond issues, create "mass protests," seek governmental intervention, distort the university (and student and faculty) image, and create the smoke by which gullible people know there is fire. It would be a great disservice to the mass media to impute the worst motives to all; but, regrettably, one can find examples of editor-politician combinations which have attempted to whipsaw universities into complete ideological subjugation, first by driving professors back into their temple and then by cleansing the temple. This aggression breeds its own retribution, indeed retribution from other mass media, but often after the damage has become almost irreparable.

The general public, with its innumerable voluntary associations, has many ways of producing consequences the university must reckon with, too. Withholding money is one potent weapon. Colleges can withstand it in theory and often do, with great flourish. They can even withstand it in practice, if it is not too much! However, activist programs which have brought faculty and students into vigorous defiance of the law, even with violence, have demonstrated that there is no accredited college or university in America so liberal in its orientation that the alumni and other benefactors will accept such defiance and disruption without verbal and financial retaliation. The provocation may have to be great, and the college officials may defend the policies or programs, but the hard fact of inevitable consequences has to be weighed in the balance — consequences which say, "There *are* bounds, and we think you are skirting or exceeding them." Parents of students or potential students have the same options and sometimes exercise them.

The most powerful public influence lies in another direction: in the capacity to influence government and to create new public policy. Every legislator has his political antenna up, and even judges and police chiefs follow the papers and the election returns. They are all helped by the interest groups who memorialize the public officials, write letters, buttonhole, and threaten. These range from the Daughters of the American Revolution to the Maoist factions, and from the National Association of Manufacturers to the Audubon Society. If the university wants to follow a tough line, the general public can be noisy but largely impotent, until it begins to speak through government.

Government has a whole arsenal of weapons, from threat to overkill. Here is where that modicum of truth in the ancient opposition to federal aid comes home to haunt us: as government has become a larger benefactor, it has gained larger capacity to injure by withdrawing its favors. Ironically, that argument was usually made by those who would have been least likely to incur public disfavor by policy disagreement. While the federal government has great and growing power to damage by withdrawal of its support, it has no ready means of singling out particular institutions. It can set standards and deny favors to those who fall short, but it has no direct appropriating capacity to retaliate as a state legislature has, and sometimes uses, over its state institutions. The power of enforcing standards as a condition of financial support is currently illustrated by both federal and state legislative amendments to bar funds to faculty and students who have been convicted of rioting on or off campus or who have willfully violated a lawful campus rule or regulation. The prohibitions could be extended to cover many other publicly offensive actions. An angry government, particularly a state government vis-à-vis a state institution, has a wide range of fiscal restraints and harrassments it can employ against the offending university, if the stakes are high enough.

Other governmental devices are police action; investigations, substantive or audit; legislative changes by statutes and by riders; admonitions in committee hearings or reports; hortatory resolutions; and formal public statements, executive or legislative. Not to be overlooked is another vast area: the intrusion of the courts into university affairs on the initiative of both private citizens and public officials. The litigious era has now hit higher education. The net effect has clearly been restrictive on the institution; and whether the university is contemplating an activist course or reacting to one in progress, it can no longer overlook how its actions may appear in the courts. Indeed, the judicial bodies, or any other of these external publics, have great capacity to agitate what might be called "the public mix," creating compounded and reinforced effects, to the serious detriment of the university. For example, the Fayette County Grand Jury in Kentucky, in one simple charge, put three "publics" on the back of "the persons in authority at the university" — by asking the Board of Trustees to "develop . . . an attitude more compatible with the desires of the alumni and general public."

So back to the troublesome question: How can

the university continue to push society toward adaptation without suffering crippling reprisal against its freedom to push? The university has the intellectual power. The public, through government, has the legal power. How can the latter be moved by the former?

Perhaps the answer is: Not at all without risks and without occasional deadlocks. Some way must be found short of surrender by either party. Society can surely find a rational ordering of its critical needs for both legal compulsion and intellectual power. Since some kind of balance will be required, opinion will inevitably enter into the striking of such balance. Burdened with that admitted subjectivity, certain guidelines, certain bounds not to be overstepped, may be suggested as a means of provoking thought as to where the balance should be and how it may be attained.

First and foremost, the university must not compromise its integrity. That is its most prized possession. Integrity sustains its claim to a role as social critic, to an outreach function, to a mediating capacity, to the public sharing of its competence, to entitlement to teach youth and to do research. It is also the most potent of weapons against the state or any other outside group in case of controversy. The university cannot afford to undermine the public's view of it as the objective searcher after truth. University professors of medicine, education, home economics, social work, nursing, and business could surely work directly in the ghettos and on ghetto problems without jeopardizing this principle. The same cannot be said for working abroad for the CIA under cover until exposed by independent sources of information. Integrity does not inhere in the problem but in the methods by which the problem is attacked; therefore, integrity does not dictate that kind of "neutrality" which really takes sides with the status quo.

Second, the university must maintain a distinction between corporate and individual views and acts. The institution is both a corporation and a collection of persons. For individual administrators, professors, and students, the university can and should vigorously defend their freedom, both on and off campus, in customary ways so far as these can be made to apply. For relief from the strain and overextension which comes from action-centered rather than thought-centered activities of "university persons" or from public-policy, decision-making involvement rather than classroom discussion, the academic community knows no way but negotiation, consideration of alternatives, appeal to mutually acceptable principles, and hoped-for agreement. If and when individuals choose to take the law into their own hands, they will have to be left to its mercies. The university cannot be a sanctuary against the law. Indeed, institutional adherence to the law might be listed as a separate guideline. It is a boundary whose parameters, particularly on the distinction between dissent and civil disobedience, have been cogently explicated recently by both jurists and legal scholars, with essential agreement. As a corporation, the university should eschew corporate positions on public policy except where its own educational interests are involved. It should otherwise neither have nor take any corporate stance simply for the sake of changing public policy. This restraint is wise because the university cannot commit, and should not coerce, its individual members. Finally, the university as a corporate body should make clear that it vigorously defends the freedom of inquiry which must be accorded to the members of the academic community and also the full exercise of that freedom, but that the institution dissociates itself from the content of such expressions and actions.

Third, the university must be free to do whatever it takes to keep relevant in its age. This legitimates the outward thrust which may cause external reprisal. Feedback from the action line is an antidote to stale knowledge. In an age of rapid change, involvement is an essential laboratory for the behavioral sciences; and direct participation may be the best way to lock professors and students onto what is relevant in their age. Despite our marvels of communication, our social environment is filled with cultures, subcultures, and varying life-styles which will remain totally foreign to both professors and students unless the ivory tower is left behind. Instructional, research, and extension programs which bring the university into better congruence with the critical problems of life are changes the university should welcome and risks the public must endure. Furthermore, this kind of relevance gives the universities grass roots where none existed before and in place of many now being torn up.

Fourth, the university must not lose its identity. It is fitted for some things and not for others. It *is* some things and not others. It has contemporary competitors unknown a few years ago — industry's educational technologists, think tanks, private corporate contractors for both education and public services, and professional bodies with educational missions. Therefore the university will have to work out a new division of labor; but that is not to say its function will shrink. The mix will be different. Selection of options will have to be made, but probably among more options. The university cannot be all things to all people; therefore, it has to decide what things it wants to be to what people. The preservation of identity means choices but not a withdrawal from the world. It means commitment where it counts and where the need and the university's competence can be fitted together. This leaves plenty of room for innovation. While institutional identity must indeed be preserved, the admonition is not to retrench but to reassess, to establish certainty, clarity, and manageability.

Fifth, the university must not lose its critical capacity. It cannot become beholden, or permit itself to be used for purposes other than its own. It cannot be an uncritical instrument for any outside force. It should not serve subjective ends under the guise of academic objectivity. It can become the agent of the government for particular, mutually agreeable purposes, but it should preserve the autonomy of shared responsibility in this particular and sacrifice none of its freedom of criticism in all other relations with the same cooperator. Obviously it can be seduced by its sources of income, but this is again, within wide and crucial limits, a matter of remedy by determination and forceful assertion. The university can be an agent of change only by the exercise of the critical competence which inheres in the specialists and the custodians of knowledge who make up the faculty.

Sixth, in its external relations the university must not seek power — intellectual power, the power of knowledge, yes; but not legal power or the capacity to coerce. That is the weapon of the state, of those who govern. The university may influence, advise, consult, aid in policy-making, serve as either agent or critic of government, and, above all, seek understanding; but when it seeks power itself, it abandons its claim to immunity from power. It should aspire to be on tap but not on top. Furthermore, to twist Lord Acton's phrase, power corrupts and academic power corrupts academically.

Finally, the university must not deny its accountability. It may be self-governing and self-regenerating, but it is self-deceiving if it denies that it owes its existence to society, with ultimate accountability to some representation of interests broader than the strictly academic. The university, like the citizen, is not a completely free agent. It is suspended between freedom and control, through that accountability which suits its peculiar social mission. Such accountability may run to the state, or it may run to a self-perpetuating private corporation, probably both through "trustees" — the ones who literally hold a trust. The strings may not be felt, the reins may be loose; but they are always there — as vague as "the demands of the age" or as explicit as a dictator's edict. The degree of activism and direct social and political involvement which will be tolerated cannot be assessed without the university's realization that there must be an ultimate bearing of the burden of defense if accountability presses the question. If the public is not to intrude into the university, what is the university's reciprocal obligation? What merits the restraint? Here again is the tightening tension. The challenge is to contain it, and to direct it constructively.

If these guidelines seem imprecise and unsatisfying, that in itself is a commentary on the current nature of university activism. It has moved from helping farmers with crops, from teaching courses off campus, and from doing what the government wants under contract, to challenging established social and economic values, to asserting moral positions, to reordering human relations, and, in some extremes, to seeking power and using physical force. It has moved from areas of consensus to areas of controversy. It has moved from operation under public policy to action to reshape public policy. The extremes in such human conflict are easy to rule out, but striking the balance in the middle is indeed a perplexity. The guidelines here suggested are standards for judgment, like reasonableness as a standard of law. They are imprecise because of the subject with which they deal. Yet the line between the permissible and the forbidden is reasonably clear. In these troubled matters, there is no escape from judgment, accommodation, and responsibility.

As John Stuart Mill said a century ago, with some unintended corroboration of the activist thesis today, observation is also a way to truth, along with reasoning. Furthermore, he said, education is fresh "to those who come to it with a fresh mind." If looking aggressively for activism, the university community might well combine this freshness of mind with the ceaseless public promotion of the idea that the free university is indispensable and that, if restrained, it would be immeasurably less useful even to those who seek the restraint. In a sense, this is the overriding activist role the university should unhesitatingly embrace: it should busy itself in so relating to, and so serving, the public — through understanding rather than power — that a majority will concede the essential conditions of such service. In this role, the university trustees have the special task of vindicating their special trust — serving as a buffer and interpreter between the university and the public. Under these conditions, one would hope to see, as a stabilizing but adaptive influence in an agitated age, the collaboration of a responsible but responsive university and a tolerant society. It takes both.

CHAPTER THREE

Governance in Transition

WHAT is happening on our campuses appears to be a power struggle among students, administration, and faculty, with the outside public joining in at various times. That, however, implies more willfulness and design than actually exists. Rather, these elements of the academic community are caught up, willy-nilly, in a sweeping reappraisal of traditional roles and goals. Student activism and arrogance pummel the administration and challenge the faculty, each of whom occasionally attacks the other for contributing to the state of affairs either by omission or by commission. All have provocation, including the students, who act more out of frustration than purpose. All are alternately pushing and elbowing, defending and rationalizing. So the walls of academe are reverberating with pandemonium rather than with the sounds of a calculated power struggle.

All the parties are being pushed by indirect forces. The chaos raises the question: "Who's in charge here?" The answer may come by muscle or by rational re-examination of the distribution of power among all claimants. In either case, change and long-term consequences are likely.

What are these indirect forces? For the most part, they are strands lost in matted heaps, but some solid threads can be identified.

One is a function of size — the growth and complexity of universities. The critics are searching for pejorative language: multiversities and megaversities. Size may generate greatly enhanced educational opportunity but effective use may depend on student resourcefulness or special institutional mechanisms to offset mass. These are too often lacking. While more than size and facelessness are involved (or there would not be even little trouble in small places), there can be no doubt that largeness, complexity, hierarchy of authority, remoteness of top officials, significant non-instructional interests, and corporation-likeness feed the fires of student discontent and arouse the nostalgia of faculty who think they remember an era "closer to the heart's desire."

Another factor, closely related, is the bureaucratization of higher education. That complication is inescapable with hundreds of employees, computerized

53

procedures, growing relations with government, larger budgets, and professional specialization. Also, combinations of institutions whose overall governance calls for off-campus "coordination" breed new bureaucracy to cope with old bureaucracies. This is not Machiavellian. It is simply the way complex entities are run; in fact, this is the internal price which has to be paid to bring focus out of diffusion and to assure adequate accountability to some governing outside public. It is also the understandable origin of levels and delegations of authority, clearances and prohibitions, and circuitous communications. Students and faculty feel that they are the special victims. The possibility that such organization can indeed mean enlarged freedom and facilitation of individual ambitions is often submerged in petty irritations.

Still another factor is the tactic of organized confrontation. Students did not invent it. They could have learned it from either big labor or big business, from "the higher moral law" or the lower ghetto, from civil rights activities or rightist or leftist politics. Students refined the tactic and applied it where never seen before — the campus. They deliberately sought an adversary posture for attention, for publicity, and for forced negotiation. Distrustful of "the system," they went outside it for frontal attack. Joining the same contagious if not endemic spirit, some faculty members mounted picket lines, went on strike, and issued manifestos. Perhaps administrators have not responded in kind because of their numerical weakness. "Having our way" by confrontation is the group counterpart of "doing my thing" by self-expression.

A potent psychological factor is the current antipathy to authority. The extreme has now been reached around the world — violence to enforce non-violent goals. The manifestations of this psychology are manifold: hostility to police, objection to parental and collegiate authority, resistance to the draft, nihilist objectives, preposterous expressions of personal freedom, and insistence on legitimating one's own social controls. Another ingredient is a new equalitarianism — everyone as good as the next, and good in all ways. Someone has called it the cult of the amateur. These are not just youthful fashions. The resistance to social restraint is in full tide everywhere. Faculty and administration also tend to breathe the same heady air — merely with more sophistication. This attitude, brooking no hierarchy, makes trouble in an age of large organizations.

This is also an age of overanalysis. The obvious has to be derived from hidden forces. Everyone is an amateur psychologist, if not psychiatrist. Alienation is a badge of merit. "Life-style" is a cover-up for irrationality — a way to "cop out" when trapped by reasoned discourse or logical relations. This is the stuff of which both nonsense and trouble can be made. It also leaves no norms for future stabilization.

Still another factor: some major decisions formerly made on campus are now made wholly or partially outside the campus. Hardly any decisions about research can be made without taking federal government funds and policy into account. Decisions on physical construction, public service both at home and overseas, and even student admissions (witness draft and scholarship legislation) are now either dictated or heavily influenced by government. Many states now have "super" boards of higher education which determine whether public universities in that state will expand, what curricula will be permitted, what new programs may be undertaken, and what appropriations may be sought. National and regional accrediting bodies wield effective sanctions and periodically must be challenged to avoid internal encroachments. Teachers' unions now aspire also to magnify their strength by making alliances to create a center of gravity outside the campus.

Finally, old allegiances are crumbling. Government and foundation grants free faculty members from university loyalty. Loans free students from parents. Administrators have always been mobile and "careerist" in the better sense of the word. The apotheosis of "feeling" frees activists from the burden of rational defense. Affluence puts everyone in a euphoria of self-conscious indispensability; hence everyone has his price.

All of these forces have had heavy institutional and individual impact. They have contributed to student disturbances, which in turn have become an independent force for fomenting the internal power struggle on the campus. It began as a student-administration battle, with sit-ins, building seizures, policy ultimatums, flouting of rules, spoiling the university's PR image, harrying deans of students, and making demands for shared governance. The faculty could view this struggle with detachment or sometimes with secret if not gleeful approval. Some professors elevated the moral level of the confrontation by sympathetic strikes of the intellect and many agreed with students that things *could* indeed be better at the top. But then the students expanded their concerns: to curricular reform, to representation in departmental decision-making, to choosing professors, to evaluating teaching, to lambasting research, to damning the immorality of professorial investigations "bought" by the government, to a shared (and often equal) role with the faculty vis-à-vis the administration. By that time, the administration was inclined to agree with the students that maybe things *could* be better at the bottom.

57

Of course, nobody really said "at the top" or "at the bottom." One implied condescension and the other superiority, when everything was really becoming leveled and homogenized. Or was it? Everything was now under attack. The old relations had become unstuck. Everyone was on the move, milling around, and a new "mix" was clearly taking unclear shape. What are the proper ingredients and the suitable proportions in university governance? That was now the question. No one in his memory, or even in his history books, could match the turmoil and the straining for some adjusted balance among the old campus forces brought to new life.

In an atmosphere as stodgy and change-resistant as a university can easily create, particularly in a period of student quiescence and faculty euphoria, these unaccustomed challenges could serve a good purpose. They could reexamine, and either revalidate or reform. Would they? Will they?

For the moment, confusion reigns supreme, maybe with some glimmerings of clarification. There is confusion of objectives. Faculty and students, as many studies have shown, have never agreed on educational ends, strangely enough; but they have not heretofore disagreed so greatly and at so many points. The university tends, therefore, to be rudderless; it lacks a coherent "why" and it has a cacophonous "how."

There is also a confusion of values. Whose values? Some want to change the rules; some want a new game. One result is a chaos of communication, which has increased both the babel of talk and the lack of understanding. As a consequence, the outside public is most confused and apprehensive of all — and no university spokesman is accorded the confidence to say what needs to be said, even if the campus were agreed on what it is.

Not surprisingly, in the current vernacular, several hang-ups occur: the faculty wants to govern without taking time from their professions, the students want freedom without taking the burden of responsibility, and the administration wants authority without taking the trouble to elicit it. Put together the indirect forces, the campus blocs produced, and the day-to-day consequences thus generated — and the status quo is bound to undergo change.

Some of the results are already becoming apparent. The university presidency is undergoing historic change. It is being weakened. Its power is being eroded. Its prestige is being undermined. It bears the brunt of almost all the critics — the students who hate "the establishment," the faculty who would have done it differently, the trustees who want a real show of executive force (particularly against activist students and unorthodox professors), and the public who are dis-

59

gusted. The president is victimized by those who hold him responsible for what they deny he has the power to do. He sits at the lonely top, where there can be only one man; but all the campus forces deny the implications of the oneness. He has shifted a long way since Lord Bryce seemed to regard him as a kind of absolute monarch. In fact, it is not yet sure that he can now become even a constitutional head, again respected because his power is *known* to be limited.

The larger the university or the governing complex of which it is a part, the more the presidency is in jeopardy. This is where more parties are seeking their "shares," more echelons permit leakages, and more valves and spigots can be opened to drain off authority. The evolution of public higher education in some of the most populous states best illustrates the point. There universities are tied together into a single system (or series of systems) under a superboard of regents or trustees, headed by an executive officer, variously called chancellor, coordinator, or executive director. Such an officer often resides in the state capital. He is a part of state government, perhaps an arm of the state's executive and a good deal closer to government than the universities are or like to be. With this new type of officer, the university president must now share part of his historic and prestigeful role. Through him, the university budget is asked, defended, and obtained (via the legislative process ultimately, of course). Through him, new degree programs are approved, new buildings obtained, and relations with sister institutions worked out. He, in short, is the state government's agent for running the state's universities — a kind of superbureaucrat. He is one with whom university presidents have to cope but certainly not one whom they want to emulate. Yet, ironically, where the "multiversity" spins off its satellite or sister institutions, producing a multicampus system all under one president (with executive officers heading each campus), the president seems doomed to become more and more like the state's "system coordinator" — removed from the campus, divorced from faculty and students, a coordinator rather than a genuine executive, a mediator rather than a decision-maker, more like a top civil servant than an influential educator.

Something similar, only much less dramatic in its pace, is also happening in universities which are private or one-campus public institutions, provided they are growing rapidly and becoming administratively complex. The president is becoming a go-between, an explainer, a front man, a fixer, instead of a scholar. He bears less and less resemblance to the professorial executive of the past. As he becomes a successful administrative specialist, he becomes an unsuccessful scholar and scholarly leader.

The current philosophies and self-assertive actions of faculty and students only compound the forces and hasten the transformation of the presidency. They create more bases to touch, more obstacles to surmount, more pitfalls to anticipate, more indecision to justify, more explaining to the trustees; and less voice in educational policy, less influence in student life, less impact on faculty development, and infinitely less assurance in articulating the university's objectives. The president is under increasing pressure to talk more, to listen more, to see more people, to designate and work through more groups — all when time has already become his scarcest commodity.

The recent heavy mortality among college and university presidents shows that this office, by virtue of its singleness, feels the greatest impact of change — greater than felt by a numerous faculty and a rapidly rotating student body. What long-run meaning this has for the effectiveness of the institution is yet to be discerned. Some articulate parties fear nothing but the premature termination of the trend toward presidential restriction, if not impotence. Others fear the loss of corporate leadership.

Two trends do seem to be predictable. Just as in industry, bigness in the university is bound to leave its mark on the executive. He will have to share more and work *through* more people and units. He will be further removed from direct and personal relation to the achievement of his organization's mission. This may require a new style of leadership but it will not mean lack of immense influence and indeed need not mean lack of capacity to make major decisions. It will mean a different *process* for making decisions. Working out that process and stabilizing presidential power at a point sufficient for accountability to the board of trustees (or other designees of whatever "public" supports the university) — this is the other trend which can be confidently predicted. The prediction rests on nothing stronger than the assumption that no multi-headed or diffuse executive model can assure that kind of accountability. If the bigness of modern organizations, including universities, militates against a self-sufficient president, beholden to no one, it also militates against those who aspire to the restoration of a town-meeting democracy or a medieval fellowship of self-governing scholars.

When all is said and done, and whatever equilibrium replaces the current turmoil, there is nothing in American culture to suggest that universities are destined to be governed without executives, and nothing in university culture to suggest the absence of need for coordination and decision-making which must culminate in a single officer. This may dictate limits unwelcome in some circles but it by no means precludes significant academic change — and that is already taking place.

While this is happening to the university presidency, what is the effect on the faculty? It does not follow that a changing presidency, even with weakening administrative and educational roles, means a correspondingly strengthened faculty. Not only must competing student claims be weighed but also the growing faculty cleavages which dilute any potential professorial gain from presidential loss. Therefore, while one net effect of the internal power rivalry will be the reshaping of the faculty role, the initial direction is less certain than the presidential evolution, and the final form is by no means yet clear. Among the forces which are still seesawing without a stabilized resultant are these, cryptically stated:

1. The student pressures on the traditional and tightly held prerogatives of the faculty, in curriculum-making, admissions, evaluation of teaching, hiring and firing, departmental administration, and determination of professional preferment.

2. Awareness that "shared" or balanced administration becomes an unwanted faculty burden when the fulcrum is pushed to the extreme and the onerous duties outrun the rewards.

3. Fear that outside masters, the ultimate char-

tering and funding sources, will abruptly close the debate about accountability and leave only the forced choice of "Through whom?"

4. Allegiance to subject-matter discipline, departmental autonomy, decisions by peer groups, and professorial entrepreneurship for grants.

5. The countervailing attraction of collective faculty action in order to amplify the unheeded voices, to regain a new coherence in place of that which has been eroded away, and even to lock arms with organized labor and the other "oppressed."

Whatever the wavering resultant of these forces settles down to be, it seems likely that faculty over the country will have a more influential but also more tightly structured role than heretofore, whether that role is grabbed by power, conceded as good administration, or negotiated calmly. University administration has to be shared, and the sharers have to be serious. The prospect for responsible sharing is now enhanced. There is a new faculty willingness born of at least the beginnings of institutional rediscovery. There is a new sense of involvement and "taking time" without fear of condescension from peers. There is a much heavier impact from the mere numbers in the profession. There are new avenues of influence — membership on boards of trustees, withholding of services, and unionization. The largest gain of all, however, and one which can hardly be escaped, will be a *clarification* of the faculty role. That is as important as *what* it is. Managerial rationalization is a crying need — allocated responsibilities, recognized channels, meshed machinery, and allowed leadership. That prospect is a casualty at the moment; but eventually it will have to be realized. Out of the current confusion, faculty and administration will have to come to terms, to break the log jams which now impede navigation for all.

Where the faculty center of gravity comes to rest in the administrative scheme of things will not hinge on competence or lack of it. That faculty trait cannot be questioned. From professors of today come the administrators of tomorrow. Certainly creativity, and even leadership, are not monopolized by any administrative officer pictured as "the leader." But faculty competence without interest, time, and responsibility is not enough. The key factors will be general faculty willingness to shoulder the responsibility — to take time for sharing policy-making powers — and the establishment of machinery for faculty representation by agents and officers who can legislate, negotiate, and advise with authority and speed. Only a shortsighted and foolish university administration, working as it must with hundreds or even thousands of faculty members of superb education and catholicity of interests, would overlook the atypical character of its managerial role and the urgent need for striking a balance between potentiality and reality in sharing decision-making with the faculty. Such symbiotic balance would certainly include effective ways of involving, hearing, and representing such personnel in their legitimate interests, both as restricted as the classroom and as broad as the institution.

No crisis of the proportions of Columbia, Berkeley, Paris, or Tokyo could fail to bring all segments of the university community into action — students, faculty, administration, and public — with contradictory impacts and with extraordinary actions and unprecedented claims. Perhaps the provocation to such action and claims was also extraordinary and unprecedented. Nevertheless, these and all lesser crises illustrate the tension points, the ambiguities, and the incapacities to govern when governance is most needed. Questions not recently asked suddenly emerge. Who has power to do what? By what procedures? Who deals with whom? Who are the decision-influencing groups and how are they linked? How are the necessary distinction and "tolerance" assured between *participating* in decisions and *making* decisions (whether made by one person or a majority)? What is the configuration of the jointness where shared concern or responsibility exists? At the end of the series of steps or at the roundup of parallel influence, what are the ultimate limits and the final resolution devices for decision-making? Answers, even if compromised and imperfect, are not only essential for academic governance but also for the preservation of any sense of community. It helps little to characterize the machinery as "hierarchical," "collegial," "participative," or "democratic." What counts is not the label but the actual machinery, the system by which it is intended to operate, and the way its participants perceive that it operates — the recognized fact, not the tag. While the requisite sorting out of roles among the campus components is at long last beginning to take place perforce, more deliberate planning could also be used.

Faculty members, like any other governing group, are instinctively united in wanting "more say." There is nothing new about this except its more vigorous articulation, which at the extreme raises the new dimension of unionism. In contrast, the student clamor is new and dramatic — something higher education has not seriously taken into account before. Some younger faculty members echo the fervor. Indeed, as more say has to be said by everybody, on more and more subjects, in the current activist spirit, the faculty finds itself seriously fragmented across the spectrum of involvement. This is also a new phenomenon.

It is illustrated in the several recent uncivil eruptions in the normally staid national conventions of the learned societies. Threats of take-over are heard. The established objectives and procedures are challenged as irrelevant. Direct action is urged. However, "taking stands," "being moral," "abandoning neutrality," "acting on your conscience" is hard on cold reason. It tends to politicize everything — to obliterate the distinctions and limitations of what is appropriate for time and place. Every relationship must be all-out. In human affairs, including the academic, only passion can produce a monolithic response; yet most faculty members are still too reason-oriented to succumb to such emotion. Hence they are divided — and, with the intensity of current activist pressures, divided as never before.

This division could be healed by either of two developments: removal of the pressures which give rise to it, or growth of mass conviction that individual decision should be forsaken for more effective group representation before a common enemy. While the most aberrant student behavior will eventually go limp out of sheer monotony, the return of the good old genteel days cannot now be foreseen. Therefore, the faculty is likely to have ample time and stimulus to cast up the balance between having the administration or the students as allies, and to decide whether the faculty's self-regarding interests are in such jeopardy that they must be advanced by hard-hitting, no-nonsense effort through faculty organization.

Hence increased faculty unionization is another possible product of the internal power shake-up. Much depends on fears. Will fears of "the administration" supersede internal divisions, and will student intrusions into faculty prerogatives also consolidate the uneasy faculty? Such consolidation might still be directed toward a common union-student target: the administration. Faculty unions have courted student alliances in time of extreme crisis — when the object of attack is the same but for different reasons — but in platforms and prospectuses, they are voluably silent on siding with the students. Teaching assistants are an exception, not because they are students but because they are teachers. Students can be union allies if they want to reform society or the administration, but they can be mortal enemies if they want to reform teaching and research or to plump for co-government. By such circumlocution, student activism may hasten the day of faculty unionization. The national pressure tends to "nationalize" the faculty response. It adds stimulus for making the administration vulnerable, undermining its credibility, and pinpointing power vacuums ripe for filling.

It is one of the ironies of contemporary higher education that unionization is now gaining appeal as the necessary *organization* answer to the deficiencies produced by years of anti-organization inclinations within the academic community. Everybody's having his say has left need for an unmistakable voice that will be heard. Every department's inward preoccupation has left need for an institution-wide view. Indeed, in public state-wide "systems," every institution's fierce autonomy has left need for system-wide considerations. So, ironically, shrewd unions are appealing to the need for order where chaos has bred. If the appeal, however disguised, offers only one extreme for another, the holders of power will at least be new.

The union retort is, of course, that unions are necessary as counterweights to vast administrative bureaucracies. Where such threatening, closed bureaucracies do exist — and no one can deny their existence even if he questions their prevalence — unions will understandably flourish. They will flourish equally where such closed bureaucracies are *thought* to exist, a strategic hint which no perceptive administrator should need. So any redistribution of campus power toward faculty organizations, however loose or tight, partially depends, on a particular campus, on how open the academic society is and is perceived to be. The struggle between professionalism and collective bargaining, with some potent implications for governance, is already apparent. Witness the reflexes of the survival instinct in the American Association of University Professors and the National Education Association.

Unhappily, credibility is one of the first casualties of universities in turmoil — everybody's credibility with everybody else.

This points to another effect of the so-called internal power struggle: the damaging blow to representation as a principle of academic governance. While a university requires governance, it is not a government in the familiar sense of city, state, or national organization. Nevertheless, like any large organization, it has to order the relationships among members in such a manner as to produce decisions and coordinate actions toward agreed-upon goals. This is where the present turmoil cuts deepest. It threatens the formal understandings and the unstated but understood rules of the game. It multiplies talk but confounds communication. It denies the necessary division of labor. It seeks to give everyone a *liberum veto* and to free him from all "imposed" authority. Everyone wallows in a sea of delightful indeterminacy. At worst, it is nihilism. At best, it is an aspiration to Athenian democracy: strictly do-it-yourself citizenship.

Unfortunately, big organizations and big universities simply will not operate that way. Instead, there must be willingness to live by group restrictions in return for group freedoms, and there must be shared responsibilities. Both require representation — willingness to let someone else make agreed-upon kinds of decisions for us and acceptance of another's services as the corollary of his acceptance of ours. This is what the current malaise either consciously challenges or unconsciously denies. But without representation, the mortar has fallen out. The organization goes atomistic — a denial of the rudimentary principle that man can vastly extend himself by ordering his relationship with other human beings, as he can by ordering his relationship to tools and machines.

The problem is dramatized by the extremist craze for "dialogue," with its threat to talk, confer, debate, and harangue the university into friction-locked immobility. While the concern, the involvement, the civic consciousness (where that is what it is) are most commendable, the fact is that in the university's circulatory system, infinite and interminable talk becomes a coagulant which produces embolisms and, eventually, paralysis. The real casualty is the principle of representation, without which no internal governance can be made to work. Sometime, somebody has to talk for somebody else, and the agent has to be able to bind his client. Implicit denial of this principle, with its ordering of duties and responsibilities, is one of the greatest current contributors to campus chaos.

The proof of counterproductivity is the eventual

cry of the talkers that they cannot "find anyone to talk to," meaning anyone with the power to listen and act. The lament may indeed be true, either because those who would formerly have acted, now being afraid of the vise between faculty and trustees, have deliberately dissipated apparent responsibility by inviting others to seem to share it; or because, under student pressure, faculty, administration, and trustees have so intertwined themselves in each other's business as to produce only more question marks after "Who's in charge here?"

The current turmoil pulls everybody into the vortex, with infinitely greater sense of involvement than sense of direction. Changes are needed to channelize involvement, to establish direction, and to mesh the gears which have become disengaged. The turmoil will have made a constructive contribution if it encourages trustees, administrators, faculty, and students to re-establish the minimal structures, to restate the rules of the game, to fix responsibilities in a division of labor, to clarify the locus and limits of decision-making for specified purposes, to provide opportunity for expressions of relevance and group interest in decision- and policy-making, and to assure institutional accountability (to some outside societal source) for adherence to its mission. The present confused state of affairs on most campuses cannot go on. A redistribution of power — whatever it is and however structured or shared — will

74

have to be recognized, agreed upon, and made the basis for carrying out the good that can come from the agonizing reappraisal born of past neglect and current turmoil.

CHAPTER FOUR

Race and Reform

Racial agitation hits the universities at their vulnerable points. University people, generally speaking, have a conscience which is already sensitized and perhaps guilt-ridden on racial matters. They are so given to learning-by-discourse that they will endure infinite verbal abuse with politeness. They are so hostile to the use of force where ideas are involved — even seemingly ridiculous ideas — that they give cover and sanctuary which the outside public would not long tolerate. Aware of their role as social critics, they are reluctant to seem to be found imperceptive or derelict in their duty. In assessing student discipline, they are sensitized to individual infractions, not mass defiance. Torn between conscience and reason, they may dissemble in response to "non-negotiable demands," leading later to accusations of bad faith. Finally, some university group with influence, if not authority, will almost certainly find its conscience so pricked by any — literally any — appeal in the name of racial justice that serious division in the academic community ensues. Racial problems, in other words, top all current campus issues in their capacity to put strains on the creaking joints of the academic machine, although it would ill become the university to be less sensitive, humane, and responsive.

The siege of the universities may, therefore, reach its turning point on racial grounds. All campus dissidents have always faced the twin questions of issue and method, and the efficacy of the latter for the former. Unlike some of the would-be revolutionaries whose strategies outrun their issues, the blacks have genuine grievances. They are left to argue about method. Too astute to be diverted or used by leftist elements, yet frustrated by conventional methods, the blacks have paralleled the major dissidents in escalating the methodology of attack. As a result, the militants soon looked moderate enough to lead. Sit-ins turned into building seizures. Non-negotiable demands became popular. One-way "communication" — the ultimatum — gained acceptance. Speeches and publications of calculated insults and of filthy language, allegedly purified by ghetto origin, became common currency. One kind of militancy polarized another kind, and each accused the other of racism. It became a foregone conclusion that

77

eventually the extremes would overreach themselves, unwittingly bringing the university to terms with its own permissiveness and indecision.

The spiraling madness reached its apogee when the most militant, sometimes in groups and sometimes individually, appeared on several campuses with rifles, pistols, and knives. The academic nadir came when university communities, although fortunately only momentarily, responded with confused indecision and debated whether even this was beyond the pale, the rules, or the law. This ratiocination soon tripped over common sense. The nature of a university is not that obscure. Openness has to have bounds. From this pragmatic lesson, universities may have found a new watershed. They may now be able to set some bounds. They may now better learn how to outlaw destruction without throttling dissent. Indeed, they may now be helped to set the conditions for institutional survival and thus to get on with the reforms which can commend themselves to university men who have surely now become socially sensitized.

This turn-about in university response to the "shut it down" extremist strategy is only one of several changes which larger numbers of black students on campus have precipitated. The catalytic influence comes from the confrontation of "the black problem" and "the white problem" in a community dedicated to reasoned change.

Universities were the scene of the first big break in racial desegregation in the South. Everywhere throughout the country, they are still the scene of agitation in race relations. They are the cutting edge of reform, although by no means always of their choice. Universities are being asked to pay a disproportionate share of society's debt to the black race. Demands that belong elsewhere are dumped at the university's door, along with legitimate claims.

But be that as it may, universities have sown the whirlwind — generally without malice but surely with colossal indifference. Their record in educating black youth is scandalous. If black youth were not often enough "qualified" for admission, the universities, as vaunted social critics, said little enough about it and did even less. As authoritative spokesmen for education, universities rarely drew public conclusions from the appalling statistics of racial disparity in university enrollments, reflecting, as it did, the alarming cumulative effect of disadvantage heaped upon disadvantage, from kindergarten to campus.

Figures for 1967 show that blacks comprised slightly more than 2 percent of the enrollment in predominantly white institutions. By 1969, they were 6 percent in all institutions, whereas they made up 12 percent of the college-eligible age group and a like proportion of the total population. The progressive nature of this conspicuous disadvantage is shown in graduate enrollment: blacks comprised only 1 percent in 1967 and less than that figure for doctoral candidates in 1969, with only 2 percent in law and slightly more in medicine. These figures obscure still grimmer facts:

1. One-half of all black students are in predominantly black institutions.

2. Consequently half are in institutions with limited occupational coverage, still with heavy emphasis on teacher preparation.

3. In law, engineering, nursing, and education, predominantly black institutions are still the major producers of black professionals.

4. There are more foreign students than native blacks in the predominantly white American universities.

5. In predominantly white universities, there is little correlation between their black enrollment and their proximity to black concentration of youth: universities in cities where blacks make up a quarter, third, or half of the population often show black enrollments of a fiftieth, a twentieth, or rarely a tenth of the total enrollment.

All this is a shocking social commentary. The disparity is quite beyond the bounds of rational defense.

Emphasis needs be placed on this as a *social* commentary first and a *university* commentary secondarily. What the university could do, by the time the cumulative effects of cultural disadvantage reached the thirteenth grade, was limited; but what the university did do, even so, was not socially responsive.

For balance and accuracy, mitigating circumstance should be noted. No one can prove that most universities were, in the past, intentionally operating on racial lines. The evidence is quite the opposite. They were operating on economic lines — inertly, unwittingly, merely admitting the youth whose economic status had brought them through high school with the required academic marks. The proof of black discrimination by inadvertence is shown by the same fate suffered by youth in similar economic circumstances, including other minority groups such as Puerto Ricans. It is also shown by the ready admission of foreign non-whites armed with scholarships or possessing independent means. In other words, the university record in educating poor youth, like black youth, has been scandalous also. On economic inequality as a deterrent to education, however, the universities have not been entirely silent, although the academic conscience has still seemed remarkably somnolent until recently. Now, monetary equalization of educational opportunity is the latest and most popular educational reform. Almost, but not quite, everybody embraces it, at least in theory. The rationale is still economic and not racial, although the black dimension has often become explicit.

Another mitigating circumstance: it is beyond the power of the university to undo in one, four, or even five years what society, the home, and the lower schools have done in eighteen or twenty years. And there is no reason why the university alone should be saddled with the total task. What the black wants, ought to have, and must get is the opportunity and education which will make race irrelevant and compensatory treatment unnecessary at the time of university entrance. He will not be free and equal until that day arrives. Helping it arrive is a legitimate and urgent university objective — indeed for all youth regardless of race.

Meanwhile, black youth have brought their identity crisis to the university campus. All factions are there — the same factions that split the black race elsewhere in society. Some want revolution, some will settle for reform. Some want symbols, some want substance. Some bank on black capitalism, some advocate world socialism. Equally divergent are the proposed strategies: some for gradualism, some for instant remedy. Agreement is on victory, not on its meaning; and some factions provide no base for communication or accommodation because they choose to "outblack" all other blacks. Unfortunately, in the current balance of forces, the militancy of the streets has come to the campus. The same militancy mans the bullhorns, talks tough, cows the moderates, and stridently issues ultimatums. It is often hard to see any other image of negritude on campus at present. In contrast, however, when concrete actionable programs are under discussion, different priorities and philosophies arise to confound university officials, who learn that there is no "black" solution to the so-called black problems.

Nevertheless, of all the forces shaking up the traditional university and shaping reform, the "black problem" may prove to be the greatest. The potency does not lie in superior leadership or strategy, but rather in the fact that the problem is stuck in our conscience, persistently remains, and has to be absorbed somehow. Its festering, its abrasiveness, its excesses only give dramatic point to nagging awareness. Racial injustice, fully recognized but only partially mitigated, is a leaden shadow which shortens the stature of everyone in the intellectual community.

By its haunting presence, the black problem challenges the traditional assumption that the university is a liberal institution. That university self-image will have to be reexamined. If general education liberalized and liberated, why had nobody asked whom and why not others? If learning made for social mobility, why had no attention been paid to who went up and who never got on the escalator at all? If the university held a monopoly on entry into all the major professions, how equitably had it doled out opportunity and how well had its resulting graduates served all segments of American society? If the academic community claimed the high prerogative of social criticism, how well had it anticipated the greatest American crisis of the twentieth century and how had it responded in its own house?

The inevitable university answer, "Race is irrelevant," only compounds the indictment. Race *ought* to be irrelevant, but was it? What in fact *did* happen? It is the practice, not the theory, which is most researchable; and universities are supposed to be good at research. How liberal is an institution which knows so little about its own illiberality?

At still another point, the black presence challenges the university as no other criticism has. It challenges the idea that an institution of higher education derives its uniqueness from being a meritocracy. Merit, yes, but by what standard? Grades? Tests? Conventionality? The challenge is twofold: whether there are not other equally or more relevant criteria which should at least be combined with time-honored tradition and whether the right objective is being served. Another appealing and competing value has appeared on the scene: equality. As a result, the social dimension of equality now has to be added to the individual dimension of merit. Awareness is at last fixed on the circularity of confining the system to those who already fit the system, thus educating the risk-free.

The raucous black demand, perhaps "non-negotiable," that blacks should be admitted to universities (generally or in black studies) "without regard to grades" challenges the other conventional extreme of "with regard to little or nothing but grades." It reshuffles the criteria. If, for example, a university promises to take half of its entering freshmen from minority groups in its immediate urban neighborhood, not from the highest-scored applicants but from a cross section of those who have made the high school hurdle, what has it done to its quality? And to its standards? The black problem rudely asks the real meaning of "quality" and "standards." Quality to what end? Standards by whose standards? Those of an egalitarian society, of possessors of talent, or of academic guardians of "the system"? Standards set by students admitted with an ever-rising level of past academic achievement (witness entering classes from the top five percentiles!), by norms in the discipline, or by predicted performance level in eventual employment? In fact, do standards consciously relate to any criteria which are explicitly meaningful to individuals or to society? Forced attention to these questions has demonstrated that there are indeed answers and combinations of considerations all too rarely considered heretofore. The new appeal of "open admissions" has put even the elitist universities on the defensive. As a result, the composition of student bodies — racially and economically, generally and in particular institutions — is undergoing revolutionary change.

Whether by black "demands" or by mere black presence, the ubiquitous race problem on campus also asks how the university harmonizes its vaunted universality with its white-European limitations and its neglect of much larger populations and much larger world areas inhabited by people of color. How modern and relevant is a center of higher learning which is so slow in heavily supplementing the transmission of a single culture, however great it is — in a country of rich subcultures and in a world of different and problem-creating peoples, both abounding in unparalleled opportunities for research and public service, to say nothing of the implications for the curriculum? University reassessment along these lines may immeasurably enrich the humanities and social sciences. The "black perspective" is not adequate either, but it will behoove the university to embrace that perspective and many other perspectives which collectively illuminate all humanity. If universities are to continue to be culture-bound, recognizing that cultural priorities are inevitable, they will be the stronger for having consciously examined *why* and having consciously determined the subcultural mix.

The blacks, supported by basic justice which "the establishment" must feel and eventually recognize, can make a university impact which ideological radicals can never muster. Even the excesses carry a message if not lost in the backlash. Therefore, the greatest query of all which implicitly faces the university concerns its purpose, mission, and justification. This goes back to fundamentals in a salutary manner not recently seen. But if the "salvation" provided by higher education is *in fact* denied to a huge segment of the American population — the disadvantaged by both income and race — the real purpose of colleges and universities is called into question. Doing what it takes to survive the system until degree-conferral, without questioning "what it takes" or how to get in, is hardly an answer. Do any concessions have to be made to serving human welfare, maximizing productivity (utilizing human resources otherwise wasted), fulfilling individual capacity, or even producing interracial comity? To what should the intellectualization be harnessed? The answer for higher education in total may be different from the answer for a particular university, but the time is obviously at hand for clearer answers for both.

Speaking of institutional variety, the predominantly black colleges and universities are in danger of being forgotten in the anxiety about "doing something for the education of blacks." The desired leverage is in the predominantly white institutions. The issue can be drawn more convincingly there. The racist-looking confrontations have to be there. So that is where the attention flows. That is where the "opening up" must take place and where access to superior quality can be gained; but the facts of where black students actually are, and will long be, should not be overlooked. Unless revolutionary change takes place there, the black higher education problem will be only half solved. Aiding black institutions could indeed perpetuate segregation, but it is too late either to begin *de novo* or to go on waiting for the ideal time for help. Remedy would seem to lie in the determination of institutional leaders, donors, trustees, and government *not* to perpetuate segregation. It is impoverishment, not new resources, that will obviate change.

Black institutions, in general, are unstable; teachers are underpaid; the best students tend to be lost to other institutions; libraries are deficient; curricula do not match the spectrum of modern careers; research funds are absent; and funds for public service are virtually non-existent. Yet these institutions have two great potentials for which modern society is eagerly looking: experience in educating the deprived and special access to persons in special need of public services. Why the federal government has been so slow in detecting these capacities and capitalizing on them is a question which appears to have, at best, an unsatisfactory answer. If it is because the institutions, in all candor, are not very good, that is precisely why the same government *is* helping universities overseas. It is hard to think of another illustration of compensatory justice which is so overdue as drastically stepped-up federal support for black colleges and universities.

The story of the black catalytic force in university life is not complete without consideration also of the current excesses of militants who so overstate their case that only a predetermined reply — in the negative — is possible. This is the opposite of the appeals to justice and conscience, coupled with drama and insistence, which have given the blacks success beyond their on-campus numbers. The university must be prepared to decode much of the gross language in which militant communications are couched, often for another audience. Something sometimes comes through. A grievance is indeed there. A horrendous case may turn out to be not horrendous but admittedly beyond defense. A long-standing practice may show up in new light, stripped of its presumed validity. But after all the decoding, translating, and discounting have taken place, many of the militant "demands" threaten not to reform but to destroy the university. Therefore, sorting out the gradations of workability and the clarity of dangers is not an easy task.

Criteria presumably should not be different from those applied to other "demands" for university reform, whatever the origin and the subject. A few obvious questions might be asked, not because there will be clear answers but because likely consequences need to be perceived and weighed.

Is the proposal compatible with the university's mission or inimical to it? As stated above, conceptions of mission are being rethought; but even so, beyond some degree of change (difficult as it may be to determine, except at the extreme, and particularly in the light of a legitimate public-service role) the university ceases to be what it professes and becomes another kind of social institution — maybe a prep school, a welfare agency, a recreation center, or an indoctrination authority. Demands have sometimes been made which make no sense by any reasonable or even strained interpretation of what a university really is.

Is the university in a position to exercise responsibility for the acts involved? Is it, and not someone else, in fact in charge? Some of the earliest proposals for Afro-American studies programs clearly sought university implementation, including finance, while shifting actual control elsewhcrc, sometimes even to student-chosen "directors" whose names would not be divulged. Permitting black cadres to recruit fellow blacks with decisions on both admissions and scholarships is another "demand" which negates the university's authority and public trust. Having Black Panthers write black history is no more acceptable than having John Birchers write American history. Unless the university preserves both control of its own affairs and use of its good name, it can easily find itself not embracing a clean purpose but locked into an ulterior one — to strengthen a faction, to buy an ally, or to injure less vocal blacks.

Can the proposal be universalized? Would it make sense if applied to everyone, or similar groups, including other minority groups? Can it be replicated? Rigid quota proposals get into trouble at this point. Does 12 percent for blacks mean x percent for Puerto Ricans, y percent for Japanese-Americans, and so on ad infinitum? Is this by colleges and departments, too? Likewise, can and should housing along racial lines be provided for other races or all races? And can ethnic curricula be farmed out to all ethnic groups? The university must be aware that the sword has another side, which may do injury to someone else.

Is the proposed change compatible with the peculiar purpose of that which is being reformed (or if not, is the new purpose indeed more appropriate)? The university may ask that question when its rule-enforcement body considers a demand for student amnesty for acts not yet committed; or when it receives an ultimatum to strip and tether the campus security force; or when it is told to divest its endowment of all "investments in evil" anywhere in the world.

No magic answers pop up for these questions, but many implications do. Every course of action has its price and requires its defense in the court of ultimate consequences. Can the university ultimately live with its decision, in its full flowering and certain replication?

Answers would be less negative if the demands were less extreme. But race on campus, in its current articulated form, is extremist; it is sometimes itself racist. Therein lie two ugly dangers. Both are escape hatches, plausible excuses, and ways around responsible action. Universities should be too wise and too humane to seize them.

The first danger is the "easy out" of pointing the finger elsewhere for remedy. The university can readily say, and has sometimes said, that the black admissions problem belongs to the vocational school or junior college; the ghetto problem belongs to government; the black employment problem belongs to industry; and on and on. What the university needs to do is to stop asking what its jurisdiction is and begin asking how it can help solve the problem. It may indeed be ill-suited, or not suited at all, for direct attack on many of the problems, but with its vaunted competence in all human knowledge, it can hardly say that it has nothing to contribute, with whatever degree of indirection is fitting (e.g., consulting instead of doing, preparing teachers instead of teaching, educating practitioners instead of practicing).

The temptation to irresponsibility, however, can best be seen by confining attention to the extension of educational opportunities to blacks. Whose job is this? Until now, it has been either unrecognized or the answer has been shuttled back and forth among educational institutions, with responsibility coming to rest nowhere, either individually or collectively. The problem has fallen through the cracks of institutional self-images and jurisdictions. Meanwhile no one can deny that *society* has a problem and a responsibility — a problem to be met somewhere, somehow. The public sector of that responsibility will have to rely on public educational institutions. It behooves such institutions, therefore, to consult and map strategy, with appropriate division of labor, to get the job done. Who takes the lead — government, university, junior college, vocational school — is immaterial; but the university is derelict in its duty if it waits for initiative elsewhere. Furthermore, it is in the university's highest self-interest to initiate action. As a college official plaintively remarked recently, the college is now presented with a bill of claims for three hundred years of black grievances. Whatever part of the bill is to be recognized and however it is to be paid, it will have to be shared among a host of social institutions according to their peculiar missions and special competencies. The university is, however, fitted for a leadership role.

The second danger lies in the accommodative mood of the contemporary university. It may let the black militant have his segregation — with incalculable cost to posterity, and particularly to other blacks. Remember that the universities once set the pattern in the rights of blacks. What irony if an American version of *apartheid* were someday to be historically attributed to the universities! And what irony for the sophomoric Bantu who might too late be surprised at how many whites are willing to "recognize" his negritude.

Every study rates racial concerns as a primary cause of academic unrest, and this is a problem which has a clear-cut campus component — about which something can be done. Therefore, race as seen on campus persistently raises questions, including fundamental, philosophical ones, which universities can no longer avoid and cannot answer except by better understanding themselves and their need for reform. Hopefully, history will eventually record that campus extremism represented attention-getting attacks on gross social ills at least then ameliorated. But in the final analysis, the most important historical judgment will be on what universities did, not with their students, but with their potential leadership for solving the problems which youthful conscience had identified.

CHAPTER FIVE

Survival and After

THE TIME has come to ponder the conditions for restoring the university to that degree of sanity and stability required for the discharge of its mission. These are conditions for *a* future, not *the* future.

Some rudimentary understanding is first necessary.

To talk of university survival, in a functional rather than physical sense, is not an exaggeration. The causes may be overaction on campus, overreaction off campus, or the resulting Kilkenny-cats phenomenon.

There are no simple answers. Some permissive campuses have become a shambles. Some authoritarian regimes have eaten their words. Most sobering of all, no university has yet come up with a model which others can rush to copy.

Universities are only one of society's institutions under tension and threat, like the churches, the corporations, the schools, the home, and the government, including the police departments. Most rocks thrown at universities come from glass houses.

The university is more the butt than the blame for most of the world's ills. Close at hand, it is the lightning rod for student disenchantment with the world.

The university is indeed a microcosm of the outside world in one sense, but the parallel cannot be pressed too far or the university loses its identity — its claim to special competence to attain special ends with special people. But the linkage between university and world is not so tight that direct university use will solve the world's major problems or that the solution of such problems will eradicate university ills. Termination of the Vietnam war will remove some causes but it will leave undisturbed the much more fundamental alienation which produces student dissent and violence also in Japan, France, India, and elsewhere.

Many activists, white and black, have written a prescription for permanent revolution — carrying on until all inequity and injustice are wiped from the face of the globe. This noble objective, like that implicit in "while any man is in prison, I myself am not free," is such a millennial star for earthlings that it is a poor basis for an ultimatum with a deadline tomorrow. The university can indeed make a significant contribution toward these ideals and it can indeed join in the "revolution" which has to be made permanent; but it should not be held hostage for solutions tomorrow.

Leaving the world aside except as an appropriate and conditioning context, and concentrating on what the university can do about itself, what are the major conditions required for restoring the torn and troubled university to its mission?

In the light of the crisis of confidence which has seized them, the first condition for most institutions is a systematic overhaul of their policy-making machinery, with a clearer division of labor between faculty and administration, leaving room for executive leadership. "Overhaul," "clearer division," and "executive leadership" require elaboration.

The pieces which lie about in great disarray cannot be put back together without a planned, systematic, methodical reexamination of the machinery of university governance. Old structures and fundamental rules — academic constitutions, if you will — must be revalidated or reconstructed along new lines. There has been enough agony, enough shaking of the foundations, enough flouting of tradition, to fuel the engines of reexamination and reform. If the sacred cows are gone, what *will* command allegiance? Since authority has to be earned, not imposed, in the last analysis

— and its power is its capacity to gain acceptance — the fundamentals of governance which will evoke such authority will have to be agreed upon. This may turn out to be something new — maybe shockingly new by the norms of the 1960's.

For example, academic legislative bodies — senates, assemblies, councils or whatever — are due for drastic overhauls, not that anyone knows of an ideal model, but new formats will have wider credibility. In the absence of confidence in the old and of knowledge of the new, candid experimentation will be in order. There is nothing sacrosanct about human conventions. We merely come to act as if there were. They can be changed more than once, in the light of experience and, predictably nowadays, in the light of changing attitudes.

Who does the overhauling may be as crucial as how to overhaul. It cannot be done by everybody in town meeting or "rap sessions." It will have to be done by representation — a manageable deliberative body officially given the task. The components or mix — proportions of faculty, students, and other groups — can be as varied as the universities themselves. But somehow the thoroughgoing reappraisal must be done. It could, in fact, be one of the most exciting intellectual experiences of the academic community. Reexamining university fundamentals, or being radical in the literal sense of going to the root, has been a great campus void for all too long. The forced rethinking of what has long been blindly accepted will also lay the basis for the necessary new consent. And, like it or not, the gears will never mesh again on many campuses until their academic citizens have had their own revolution, in their own time, and created constitutions better to their liking.

That a clearer division of labor is needed between faculty and administration does not preclude reform in the role of students. If the constitution-makers want to deny the validity of the distinction between professionals and amateurs and assert the equality of faculty and learners in the university's total business (not only instruction but also research and problem-solving), then they can do so and frame a constitution accordingly. However, the assumption for the present here is that while education may be too important to be left to the educators in one sense, it also requires too much training, experience, skill, and single-mindedness to be shared equally with alumni, public, or students. If that is the case, there is still the question of the role of and relations between those who directly teach, do research, or provide off-campus services and those who indirectly affect the same by their facilitative (administrative) responsibilities. The directly related and facilitative groups cannot, in the nature of things, have the same functions; and the trouble begins when functional differentiation and relationships are indeterminate or fuzzy.

An organization is either so simple that it has no differentiation of function — and hence no officers doing anything *through* others — or it is sufficiently complex to justify a division of labor. When the latter stage is reached, it is a contradiction in terms to say there is a differentiation of functions without clarity or identifiable differences. Webster says differentiation is "an alteration yielding a characteristic difference." Yet that is precisely the problem in university governance, generally speaking: those who can and do make education possible, through a complicated interlocking of professional competencies, are not sufficiently clear about their expected spheres and agreed-upon limitations. The total university job long since has been subdivided; so it is folly to keep on acting as if all functions were homogenized and everybody could deliver the university's total services singlehanded.

It will not help the academic constitution-makers to attempt to justify the customary fuzziness by saying academic power is peculiar in that it must be shared. Indeed it must, but even shared power has to be shared on some explicit terms — and sharing does not imply that all sharers do the same thing. The sharing may be individual-with-individual, individual-with-group, or group-with-group, and the important thing is that the relationships have been thought through and made both orderly and understood. Needless to say, the relation between teacher and accountant or researcher and legal counsel is not likely to call for the clarification that is needed between professor and dean or senate and president. It is the academic process or continuum that causes confusion, as illustrated by educational policy-making, decisions on professional preferment, and budget-making. As discussed later, student discipline has become another murky and contested area in recent years, thanks to evolutionary delegations from trustees to president, president to faculty, faculty to committee, or other variations, now half taken back or rendered nugatory by unanticipated student behavior *en masse*.

While the roles of differentiated functions and the jobs of persons performing such functions can be defined at the center, and on a by-and-large basis, areas of overlap and confusion are bound to remain; and no constitution or charter can anticipate and resolve all questions, for that would be to confuse government with constitution. The in-between areas have to be covered by machinery for resolving the confusion, by some prearranged guidelines and standards, and by an orderly, understood way of getting a decision. Such fundamental reexamination and reordering of the structures and relationships of the academic community are overdue in most universities — to yield a better form of governance, to be sure, but also to force attention and elicit involvement, to reeducate academic citizens on the conditions of institutional survival and professional freedom, and to restore confidence in the processes by which the university seeks to live and work. The gains will be, and ought to be, both substantive and strategic.

It was suggested above that such probings and reforms should, however, leave room for executive leadership. This is in no sense to suggest that leadership can be decreed; it merely suggests that leadership should not be precluded or, rather, that it should be left uninhibited if not facilitated. It should be left open for exercise when such talents show themselves. There is a legitimate and essential executive role in university life, as there is a legislative role — just as in government, the organized church, or any other complex institution. And in all institutions, too, certain experiences tempt executives to think ill of legislators, and vice versa, to the point that each may at some time wish to dispense with the other. This attitude is not unknown in the universities, but it is a psychosis which must be remedied. Toleration of the executive, to say nothing of according him a necessary role in university affairs, comes hard for some academics because they are contemplative and want the university to be contemplative to the point of total immobility — no action to ruffle the philosophical calm. A certain student companion piece avers that presidents and their ilk should simply keep the classrooms clean and the pencils sharp. This overlooks the possibility of further reduction to absurdity: Mark Hopkins and the student at the other end of the log did not need a housekeeper at all.

A revealing test would be the consequences of wiping out all governance and all functional titles in a large modern university. The hundreds or thousands of members would then have to begin asking some sober and sobering questions. By what means would the university now have any working relationship with the outside, public and private — for students, for money, for freedom, for survival? How would resources be distributed internally? How would professional interests be identified, presented, and acted upon? How would all the groups that want action arrive at either a plan or a consummated decision? How would a university-wide view be assured and articulated? How would the rudiments as well as the amenities of academic discourse be preserved against hostile internal elements? In other words, it would soon become obvious to all but anarchists that a division of labor, an ordering of responsibilities, and an institution of a system of authority would have to be devised; officers would have to be named; and, ultimately, an officer-of-officers would have to have some kind of final say, however hedged-about the conditions might be.

A university needs many kinds of leadership — in every discipline and unit, from bottom to top; and it gets too little of it in most cases, both because leadership is a rare quality and because the present campus environment discourages it. Institution-wide leadership is both academic and managerial, and while there is ample opportunity for both faculty leadership in academic matters and administrative leadership in managerial manners, there is still the question of the ultimate centrality at the confluence — the single executive whose scope is institution-wide. The present-day university needs to concede his indispensable role, to reinstate him, and to give him unmistakable authority *at his appropriate level* (or his agreed-upon sphere, if hierarchy must be avoided). Of course he should be given the sensible constraints any executive should expect; but the indispensable requirement is that the system *permit* him — if "encourage" is too strong — to exercise leadership.

Leadership cannot be legislated; it grows from being exercised. Indeed, little of it is being exercised in universities today, essentially because it is not "permitted" in the sense of favorable or accepting attitudes among potentially vetoing academic groups. Presidents themselves have not been blameless in playing the "participatory" game, wherein they are amiable comrades treading lightly and waiting for signals. A popular outside conception which yearns for the old schoolmaster tyrants is equally deplorable. No Moses can or should be expected; but the academic community in all its parts can be immeasurably helped by an institution-wide view based on system-wide sources of information, a high arbiter of views and actions, a spokesman who can lift sensible ideas to high visibility (whether his own or some internal consensus, or an innovative trial balloon); a respected liaison with the outside world; and one who himself believes leadership is to be exercised, not awaited.

In the reexamination and reform of university governance, there will have to be a return to representation as a central principle, as asserted in an earlier essay. The chaotic do-it-yourself approach, based on endless and sometimes mindless "rapping," on participation as an end in itself, and on contempt for hierarchy and actionable finality, simply will not permit a large organization — even one as proudly amorphous as a university — to survive under attacks, let alone to function. An organization has to have the capacity to "make up its mind" prior to action, like an individual. It can be done by head count on every matter and every facet of every matter, or it can be done by having someone or some manageable group take the responsibility for, in place of, and on behalf of the ones who might otherwise have been polled.

It is a favorite theme of many activists that representation is an antique, outmoded idea, like "liberal," "reason," and "neutral." They have pressed the point so far that the principle will indeed be hard to reactivate, because it rests on consent and willingness to be bound by actions of surrogates. Without the willingness, implicit in the attacks on the principle itself, nothing is left but anarchy at worst and direct democracy at best. "Participation" is the new hope. However, if the point is legislation, surely not all can do it directly. If it is consultation, surely not all students can consult the faculty or administration, nor can all of the latter simultaneously be consulted. The catch to participation as a substitute for representation is the absence of real intention of making decisions, with binding effect and accountability for the result. The spirit is one of perpetually stirring the cauldron but never casting the molten materials into forms or extruding them into decisions. Yet the companion piece of participatory advocacy is an intense drive for immediate reform — that is, decision and action. With the principle incapacitating the objective, the ground is laid for frustration, complaints of bad faith, bitterness, and, for the extremists, violent guerrilla action "outside the system."

The extent of the deterioration of this aspect of governance is illustrated on all sides of academic life. A student stands in an international university assemblage and says, "This professes to be a congress of universities, but only presidents are here." (The same could be said if only students, professors, deans, alumni, donors, graduate assistants, or janitors were there; so apparently any bona fide university meeting must include all of them.) A self-appointed student group solemnly assembles to "repeal" all existing student regulations and codes of conduct "inherited from another generation." A reform faculty group insists that the university senate as an elected fraction of the faculty is obviously not the faculty and cannot act for it. An "indigenous leader" demands equal voice with the duly elected president of the student body because "sand-box government" is unrepresentative. A black leader contends that the curriculum, made and approved by whatever men and women of erudition in whatever fields, is irrelevant until made by blacks for blacks. A strike-advocating group says, "We went through all the channels, every one, but still a stupid 'No.' " All this adds up to a blueprint for total participation — with aborted action. It is a game of perpetual huddles; the ball is never snapped.

When, at last, the common sense of representation is again perceived, choices will have to be made among the many possible forms needed. Different organs of governance will call for different modes of representation, as will the vital interests of the constituent groups in the academic community. Different interpersonal and intergroup relations, with different objectives, will also call for different kinds of representation — depending, for example, on whether the mode of action is legislation, consultation, negotiation, or participation.

Faculties as well as students are involved in this rehabilitative process. The faculty has not arrived at the student contempt for representation, but it has been prone, on the one hand, to personal involvement as a condition for policy acceptance and, on the other hand, to a compromise with reality, resulting in the proliferation of committees upon committees in time and hierarchical sequence which not only wears down the issue but also wears out the participants. The general absence of "academic statesmen" nowadays has often been noted and regretted; but leaders do not easily arise among those hostile to being led or hostile to machinery through which leadership can function. Faculty scholars who become interested in institutional policy formulation tend to be put off by procedures which require *de novo* consideration of issues in each of a series of committees and each of the levels of hierarchy. The faculty problem with representation, unlike the student problem, is only partly one of acceptance and largely one of finding effective forms. In the current crisis, institutional survival is dependent on faculty attitudes and actions, and particularly on dependable and effective means of getting a faculty decision or consensus upon which executive action can be grounded on behalf of the institution. However self-sufficient if not complacent it might have been in quieter times, the faculty, facing the bellicose mood of the outside world, will have to have something done *for* it and on its behalf. The question is how to identify or formulate the "what" which must precede the "for."

Agreement upon a viable means of representation is also a method of creating authority in the academic community — authority to be used and respected for its use. It is a mode of eliciting consent. Authority to take action in the interest of the university with by-and-large consent of the university community is the missing ingredient today. That is why a reexamined structure and procedure, with whatever reform is acceptable to the participating groups, is needed on many if not most campuses. That process itself will force a restatement of institutional aims and build the basis for consent. Universities need to be clearer on what game they are playing and by what rules.

A caveat is in order: obviously the fundamental machinery of governance advocated here is not conceived as a monolithic channel through which all university business and interest must flow. There is plenty of business and interest which is not of an institutional decision-making variety, including the learning within classrooms and laboratories; so there is a place for a rich variety of other forums, organizations, and modes of expression. They may have little to do with the governance structure or they may undergird it by generating views which seek representation. Much of the immobility and impotence of universities have come from confusion between these two: the university organized (or *un*organized) for contemplation and the university organized for decision. They cannot be divorced, but they call for peculiarly appropriate, and very different, tools. The circularity and timelessness of contemplation does not facilitate decisions. "Hierarchy," "authority," and "representation" may be anathema in certain academic circles nowadays, and certainly the labels do not matter if more palatable ones can be found ("organizational linkages," "consent systems," etc.); but decision-making requires deliberation from an information base, with a progressive narrowing of the options until action can be taken in a limited time frame — and ultimately taken by *somebody* properly empowered. This applies to both legislative and executive matters, however different the forms.

When the structural reforms are agreed upon and representation is incorporated as a participatory device, the new role of students in such governance is bound to arise. This is a place where reform can be and ought to be more radical than anyone would have dreamed a decade ago. The burden of proof has now shifted from students who want to participate to those academics who think it inappropriate. Extensive experience in recent years has proved that the worst does not happen when students are included in academic bodies. They are more responsible when taken in than when put out, and the "consumer" point of view needs to be heard. They best learn when they are motivated, and presumably they are motivated when they readily challenge so much of the conventional wisdom about universities and their operation. This is both a fitting environment and the appropriate stage for "learning" to take place between challengers and challenged. At the violent stage, resort to "learning" is only a guilt-derived substitute for punishment.

Therefore, whether one proceeds from educational grounds or strategic grounds, the outcome is the same:

it would be wise to give students a greatly enlarged voice. That voice might be largest in student-oriented matters and smallest in what is furthest removed from student knowledge or interest, but the times call for some kind of significant and broadly based student representation on a university body which can address itself to institutional aims, plans, and policies. The student voice, student concern, and student interest should be heard and felt so that students and others may educate themselves in the resulting give-and-take. This is one way to respond to the crisis of understanding. Whether this moves from the forum to full-fledged legislative functions will vary from campus to campus; but all parties must be clear on limitations, on expectations, and on the system of representation. Students do not know more than the faculty and they cannot do more than full-time academic officers; but new roles should be tried — and changed if they do not work.

Students may well have won more than they can make good on, whether on grounds of skill, time, transience, or sustained interest; but if so, they can best be convinced by experiencing the points of failure firsthand. This kind of reform does not put the university in jeopardy, or need not if properly safeguarded by a balance between influence and power. Clear-cut concessions here are far better than mincing and grudging concessions which create confusion or divide responsibility at still more critical points, such as in the judicial processes by which the institution protects itself against disruption or shutdown.

That raises another critical condition for university survival and for renewed hope. However absurd talk of survival may sound a few years hence, as one would ardently hope, the word is not too strong now, in view of some student manifestos, some faculty collusion, many campus bombings, myriad threats of "shut it down," and backlash with reprisal among the public. Therefore, universities must find better ways to protect themselves against disruptive acts, particularly on a massive scale. This is not easy, given the fragility of an intellectual institution based on reason, mutual confidence, and a desire to make all student experience educational. Some clues are found in what has been learned negatively:

1. The old student rules based on individual misconduct toward individuals are not adequate for acts directed against the university or against society.

2. Student courts or student-dominated disciplinary machinery is not effective against students who invoke political and anti-authoritarian motives.

3. The old dean's summary dismissal has been superseded by the new "due process" which must fulfill the requirements of the courts.

Therefore, where mass disruption and violence are involved, universities need to reshape their disciplinary procedures and tighten them up for rapid action and fair trial outside the student subculture. Universities may revamp their judicial processes by options which run from machinery less subservient to students, through administration-dominated processes, to an independent judiciary outside the existing structure of the university (e.g., a judge and hearing officers appointed to deal with cases *for* the university). More important than particular forms are certain ingredients: clarity of rules and procedures, pinpointed responsibilities at every stage and cohesive direction at the top, speed of action with appropriate sanctions, "due process" as defined *by* the courts but not like that *in* the courts, and credibility — that is, a system which is fair and is seen to be fair. Clarity, speed, and certainty are sorely missing on many campuses now. A university which has the professional competence to advise society on the reform of the administration of justice should get its own house in better order.

Similarly, a fresh look should be taken at the means by which faculty and other staff members accused of violence or disruption can be dealt with fairly, speedily, and with balanced regard to internal and external interests. It is regrettable that the university has to cope with a new phenomenon: its own employed members, fortunately a minuscule minority, who resort to direct acts of violence and coercion to work their will on their colleagues and on the institution to which they belong. As the old individual rules are inadequate for riot control among students, so the old academic freedom procedures are often inadequate for dealing with internal challenges to the rudimentary functioning of the university. If the old procedures can be retreaded or otherwise made to work, so much the better; but candor requires some recognition of the fact that inward-looking groups are poor policemen over themselves and might, both in self-interest and out of regard for a larger public, invoke some objective assistance. Whoever regards this as an offensive and unnecessary kind of professional self-appraisal and self-denial bears the burden of proof that the current extremes of faculty action (as distinguished from expression) are neither unprecedented nor threatening to institutional survival.

Reforms in these directions for both students and faculty are urgently needed, plus a willingness among all elements of the university community, including faculty, to *use* the machinery, or have it used, once set up. This calls for faculty and administrative willingness to distinguish between dissent and disruption, to regard perpetrators of violence as beyond the therapy of "turning it into a learning experience," to

punish violence done under the cloak of political sym-
bolism, to see colleagues disciplined if guilty, and to
sanction the use of force in extremity. That is the pill,
formerly bitter but now sweetened a bit, which will
have to be swallowed before the university's malady
will pass. This is not a tough policy. It is merely a
sufficient policy — sufficient without going to the simplistic extremes advocated by public men who have
their own Augean stables to clean in violence in the
streets, markets, and battlefields.

A subtler kind of threat to the university, but one
with devastating potential, is the drive to use the university as an instrument of public policy — to inter-
vene overtly and aggressively for social change even
where, or perhaps particularly where, political resolution of the issue has not yet taken place. This is the
threat of politicization. It enjoys great current popu-
larity, and it has ardent supporters in great numbers.

Once the agent-of-change role of the university,
or its social-criticism role, or its public-service role
is embraced, the highway to politicization lies ahead
if the turn is abrupt enough. No one need travel it
to the end, but many are doing so — some clear-eyed
but many more because they mistake their destination.
Hence "the university" (presumably as a corporation
and a congeries of groups) must "take a stand" on
every public issue, "put its weight" at the right places,

and vigorously exercise its conscience — not only to stop the war in Vietnam, to eradicate pollution, and to end racism, on a national scale, but to strike locally for peace, to boycott a local factory until its effluent is cleaned up, and to whip the city council into line on housing, employment, and human rights. Unquestionably the university has a role to play in these great and pressing issues, with their pervasive local manifestations, but not to the point of preempting or rivaling the role of politics and government. The university is one of society's specialized and limited institutions, and it is secure only in adherence to that for which it has peculiar and recognized competence: knowledge and its uses.

As an institution, the university can and must attempt to distinguish between its legitimate involvement through its public service and the impropriety of a role normally reserved for public policy–making bodies (political parties, lobbying pressure groups, legislatures, and elected executive officials). The university itself must make the distinction — and without being ordered, pressured, or bought. It must distinguish between the uses of knowledge and the uses of power. Where to draw the line is the essence of all discretion, and university officers exist for that purpose. Trying to relieve them of trouble is no excuse for the university to return to its ivory tower. The

other major university missions — teaching and research — also call for drawing lines, on what not to
teach and on what research to let alone. Such decisions are also difficult; they differ in that they are not,
generally, quite so exposed to public scrutiny and partisan interest. But even on matters of such scrutiny and
interest, there is plenty of room for involvement which
is objective and detached rather than partisan, and for
service which is knowledge-based rather than power-
based. The modern university cannot be like the Ben-
gali intelligentsia who are oblivious to Calcutta.

The overly enthusiastic activists overlook a simple
fact: more than one faction can play at the same game.
If the university is to be used, there will be more than
one user; and it is a foolish activist who believes that
he can have the campus to himself — either for his
ideas or for his kind. The great seal of the university
cannot be carted off without contest from some quarter. Therefore, every issue will have to be threshed
out and voted out, if not literally and physically *fought*
out, before the university can express its conscience
or wield its political clout. The activist cry of outrage
at the retaliation of the "hardhats" and the blacklash
of the rightists is the first evidence of sophomoric
education.

The result for the university is its conversion into
a political battleground with no pretense of neutrality,

unless established by deadlock, and no concern for credibility. While many groups can play the game of politics by democratic rules, no more than one group can play the authoritarian game of coercion without clashes and eventually violence. When opposing commandos engage in university hijacking, a crash is imminent. So the current move toward politicization of the university, with much innocent simplistic support, often girded in moral outrage, is an internal threat of major proportions.

Action produces reaction; the threat on campus in turn breeds political retaliation from the outside, with the long arm of interference, the loss of autonomy, and the steady march of intrusion upon intrusion. The screws of politicization are thus turned another round, with one kind by the activists, another kind by the politicians, and the university *as an institution* the loser on all counts.

This is a danger from which the university must protect itself. Little is required except conviction and courage, but these are grounded in that which is now in remarkably short supply: institutional awareness. In times of less stress, the traditional posture of most academics has been awareness of and loyalty to something less than the university — the particular office or laboratory, the special discipline, or, rarely more, the home department. The total university is now under attack, both from within and from without, and there is some encouraging evidence that academic man is beginning to perceive that what he prizes and depends upon, although heretofore taken for granted, is inextricably tied to the fate of his university *as an institution:* his very position, his having students to teach and research to do, his needed funds, his tenure or other claims to professional freedom, and the total environment of his career. In the fury of the storm, it is less attractive than formerly to believe that a professorship, a discipline, or a department is an island unto itself.

The task of university rehabilitation also partially hinges on the rediscovery of the institution and the reestablishment of institutional identity — the lifting of sights and awareness above the sub-institutional and extra-institutional concerns. This is neither vacuous loyalty nor romanticism. Instead, it can have a solid intellectual base: the appeal of an intellectual home which is surely not less than the many respected disciplines it houses. It is not expecting too much, therefore, to hope that the reexamination of mission, the reform of governance, and the rethinking of program will help to develop a sense of common goals, of mutually supportive ideals, of a trust to be carried forward, of something worthy of defense against attackers, and of values which will still be cherished by society when properly presented. Presidents, deans, and other administrative officers have too long lamented and blamed others for the phenomenon they have done little to change. Change now appears possible and it can be immeasurably hastened by leadership which refines institutional goals by attempting to articulate them, convincingly mediates between institution and public, and sounds the call to arms when dangers portend institutional disaster.

Faculty, students, and administration are being attacked institutionally. They need to respond institutionally, not for bureaucratic reasons but for intellectual ones. This is a rare opportunity to close ranks, to substitute a major issue for minor ones, and to undertake the task of reestablishing the public credibility of the university, which is now a punching bag for gleeful politicians because it has lost its capacity for institutional recoil. The university offers no effective rebuttal to simplistic solutions publicly proclaimed for its problems — not that the case is not there, but rather that sub-institutional concerns shout louder than the muted voices of common cause. The university will be in deep and desperate trouble until faculty, students, and administration awake to the insidious nature of public proposals to screen professors politically, to finance teaching as the sole university function, to remove the making of educational policy from the campus, and to put purifying strings on student and institutional finance. These are axes laid at the root. Therefore, the remaking of institutional consciousness and its use for both defense and change are long overdue.

As so often happens in human affairs, adversity breeds remedies, and crises generate new energies. When the university establishes the conditions for survival in its hour of greatest trial, it will have stepped on the threshhold of a new era. It will have made itself again ready for advance, and it can be the stronger for its agony.

However, the forces of challenge — even the violent manifestations — will require more than containment. The university's survival and rehabilitation must be *for* something. Beyond the reconstructed minima and redesigned fundamentals, the substantive educational program is what matters — how better to harness youthful ideals and conscience to societal reality and how better to extend and relate knowledge to human problems. The reexamined university will need to provide something new. Its targets are moving. Its relevance is inconstant. The instruments discussed here have to be applied to something; and the devising of that something is the agenda ahead for faculty, students, and administration — at last engaged in the planning and execution of a common mission. The substance of that mission can then again receive the attention which its centrality deserves.

Among the "something new" most urgently needed are more effective means of program evaluation and more assured means of educational innovation. Going on as in the past, without periodic revalidation of policies and programs, is an ancient university weakness. University professionals are like all others — myopic in things professional and attentive to self-criticism only under outside pressure. There is need, therefore, for internal research and critical evaluation — for knowing the facts, for sharpening the issues, for posing the questions, and for stating the alternatives. This is a task for skilled research personnel, but it is more than that: it must have another dimension which can only be supplied by seasoned academic practitioners whose time and talents are invoked for guidance, broad-gauged vision, and wisdom as a check on mere information analysis. This new dimension, with greatly increased emphasis and funding, should be added to the inadequate old idea of institutional research, so that the reinforced combination can keep the academic community keenly and perpetually aware of what experience shows, of what others are doing, and of options worthy of consideration — plus helping answer other questions which the alerted academic community is stimulated to pose.

Also, the needed companion piece is built-in innovation. Change pervades a live university. It cannot
be put off in a corner by itself, yet there is a need to
institutionalize innovation somehow. It is neglected
otherwise: everybody's business becomes nobody's business. Of course it is folly to assume that innovation in
education is limitless and that some sudden, blinding
breakthrough will obliterate the past. There are many
alternatives between Mark Hopkins with his log and
Clark Kerr with his multiversity, but recent studies both
in America and in the new British universities indicate
that the rhetoric of innovation has outrun achievement. It is sobering that daring models of sweeping
substitutes for the past are not in evidence. Within this
context of the need for realistic and incremental progress, some group in some office under some officer
should make innovation its special business, not that
any such persons can be all-wise but that nothing less
will provide either the needed focus or the challenge
to superior wisdom, if that can be aroused. The need
is for staff work which can be bounced off the minds
of those who are challenged and whose concurrence
is necessary, and for all kinds of ad hoc utilization of
special faculty expertise. Whether the proverbial wise
men inhabit universities, there are surely men uncom-
monly wise about the university's own internal business. Better means are needed to elicit their talents

in application to what is so familiar that vision may otherwise not be lifted above the dusty, well-trodden path.

A built-in rolling assessment of status and of plan for change — that is, institutionalized evaluation and innovation — may produce some controversy and even some trauma, but it can also be both a safety valve and a guarantee of better adjustment to the generation to be served. It can present, for a change, the right kind of confrontation: between universities and their unexamined educational alternatives.

Universities may be in a bittersweet era, but few of us would romanticize that this is both the best of times and the worst of times. The worst has gained the upper hand, and it will take some doing to break the grip. Yet the prospects are bright. Universities may indeed have to begin a new set of worries. If not campus disorder, then what in its place? If the drums of dissent subside, will higher education give evidence that it has listened not only to the shrill dissonance but also to the deeper beat beneath? If the spirit of activism wanes, whether from fatigue or frustration, can the youthful conscience and ideals be saved from an incoming tide of indifference or cynicism? Youth are the latest model of the human race. They are our link with the future; their enemies are our enemies. If they do not control the universities now, they will when the most important generation gap — that within themselves — is closed. Even their stridently asserted half-truths will help us to see that the assumed whole truth is only half right.

Therefore, it is too early to despair. Universities *can* pull themselves together.